Here's Why **You** Can't Find **Love**

Written by Ted Santos
Edited by Leasa Simmons & Stacy Padula

Copyright © 2021 Ted Santos. All rights reserved.

This is a work of fiction. Names, characters, places, and incidents are either a product of the author's imagination or are used fictitiously, and any resemblance to actual persons, living or dead, business establishments, events, or locales is entirely coincidental.

No part of this book may be reproduced or transmitted in any form or by any means, graphic, electronic, or mechanical, including photocopying recording, or taping without the written consent of the author or publisher.

Briley & Baxter Publications | Plymouth, Massachusetts

ISBN: 978-1-954819-04-7

Book Design: Stacy O'Halloran
Cover Design: Mackenzie Wells
Cover Art: Maddy Moore

Preface

My Genesis

Before I dive into this wildly interactive conversation, I would like to share a little about myself. As a very young child, I preferred sitting with the adults while the other children played outside. I would hear my uncles talk about women. They would often say women should come with instructions. That stuck in my head. As a child, it sounded as though men were complaining about being unable to understand women. To assure that I did not fall into the pit of complaints, I came up with a background solution. At nine years old, I decided I would be the guy who understood women. I even thought I could write the instruction booklet for other men to read.

At nine, I read books about sex, female anatomy, Q&As from women with a psychiatrist, and miscellaneous magazines that talked about the things women want from men. The Q&As were particularly interesting because the questions came from real women with important concerns about sex, dating, challenges with men, and understanding a woman's body during sex.

By twelve years old, I was certain that any woman who spent time with me would find me irresistible. In fact, I would look at couples and think to myself, if she spent time with me, she would forget his name. Also, at eleven, I started to train my body through serious exercise. I wanted a body that was physically appealing to a woman—and I wanted my body to perform during sex like no other man.

So, from the age of nine, I not only read books and magazines, but also interviewed friends of my mother and aunts. I wanted to confirm my findings in the research I had done. I continued the mindset of interviews throughout my teenage years. It also spilled over into my dating life. By fourteen, it seemed that it would be in my best interest to study human behavior in general—men and women.

If you guessed there is a flip side to being well informed, you are right. Through my research, I had become mature beyond my years. That left me as a fourteen, fifteen, or sixteen-year-old who was much more mature than the girls my age. As you can imagine, not too many seventeen-year-old girls are interested in a fourteen-year-old man-boy. Even my freshman year of college was filled with situations where upper class women told me I was too young. They did this despite already having an affinity for me. It was not until I was nineteen that I was able to date women in their late twenties and thirties.

Nevertheless, in college, I continued my research through books and interviews. Of course, I found psychology courses interesting. What I found more interesting was economics. Economics is sociology with financial components and mathematical equations to predict human behavior.

While economics intrigued me, my major was marketing. For me, marketing did not predict human behavior. It shaped it in masses. To do that, you had to understand mindsets and current desires of people. With marketing, you can make people desire things they did not know they desired. Look at the cell phone, especially the iPhone.

At some point in my late twenties, I had already gone through a string of, what most would call, successful relationships. While they were successful, they were "just good." I was after more than "good."

In the meantime, my professional life became the center of attention. I became a sales trainer. I worked for Sandler Sales Institute, and that job was more than a career. It expanded my desire to learn about people. They focused on the psychology of sales. For me, it was a perfect match for the man I had become. The methodologies I learned were designed to uncover what people really wanted or what they wanted to avoid. It was especially good for handling acrimonious prospects.

Sales training supported my next career move, which was an executive for a rapidly growing transportation logistics company. At this point, I was living with a woman for the first time. As a woman, she was great. I met her when she was in law school. So, it was fair to say I could use logic to reason with her. Much of my research about women was extremely useful in maintaining a good relationship with her.

As a woman, she was supportive of my career. She was a great sounding board for me to talk about any challenge at work. As a result, I excelled in my career and made a decent amount of money. That allowed she and I to travel throughout the United States and abroad together. In addition, in my professional life, my research in human behavior and sales training was instrumental for me being able to empower people in an enterprise that was going through growing pains. For the first time, I felt as though all my skills and knowledge were being used. It was a great time for me. There were times that I hated the weekends. The weekend interrupted the fun I was having at work.

After five years of living with this woman, I pursued a childhood ambition. I left the United States to live abroad. For two and a half years, I went through eight countries: Belize, Panama, Costa Rica, Nicaragua, Guatemala, El Salvador, Honduras, and Mexico. I traveled from one country to the next by plane, bus, boat, and horse.

I lived in cities, jungles, and small villages. I even lived with Mayan Indians in the jungles of Belize with no electricity or running water.

Not only was this adventure a personal aspiration. It continued my studies in human behavior. It was amazing to see that people were people no matter where I went or the language they spoke. I was also able to see a new and empowering perspective on community. In the United States, communities are obliterated from divorce and crime. In the jungle, in villages with 330 or 550 people, I experienced community in a way big cities have not been able to replicate. I also saw how people collaborated when money was not a motivating factor.

When I returned to the United States, I had $55 to my name, and it was borrowed. It was January 15th, 1999, and I was here as a pit stop. I was going to make money and leave the country again. However, I eventually found myself being an entrepreneur. I later sold the business and worked for a consulting firm that specialized in transforming behavior and corporate culture. I was fascinated with this even more than the sales training. The training in this consulting firm was like a language of its own. Some of the methods matched what I had discovered through my research and experience. Except, they had done more research and were much more sophisticated than me.

This next phase of my career took me down a much-desired path. I was now positioned to train, develop, and advise leaders of organizations. Everything I learned from human behavior, as well as being an executive, became part of my tools to service clients. I became an advisor to CEOs of midsize to large companies. I built boards of directors, changed corporate culture, and helped them execute breakthrough initiatives.

Through this training, intimate relationships became even easier. By now, I had dated countless women and decided to live with a beautiful South American woman who was twenty-one years younger than me. The first cohabitation lasted five years. The second was three.

Here's Why You Can't Find Love
The focus of this book is love relationships. However, the principles are relevant to any relationship. This work stands on the shoulders of a methodology that is designed to help people or organizations produce breakthroughs in their relationships. The heart of the book revolves around one question: What would be a breakthrough in your love

relationship? It shows how a breakthrough in your love life can have reverberating effects in every aspect of your life.

I was invited to a celebration for someone I have known for decades. She invited about twenty-five of her friends and employees. I was the only man. After most of the women left, there I sat amid five women. Throughout the night the conversations were general and pleasant. At some point, it became very focused on relationships. They wanted to hear brutal honesty from a man's perspective—an honesty that could only be conveyed with a high level of comfort and trust amongst the six of us.

This story is an interview of me, Ted Santos, by five women: Susan, Tasha, Andrea, Kelly, and Leslie. Of the five, Susan is the one I have known for many years. Kelly and Leslie were strangers. I had met Tasha and Andrea on one other occasion.

As a word of caution, the content of this conversation can easily be considered counterintuitive. The challenge with counterintuitive conversations is you will be tempted to understand it through that which you already understand. In fact, it is safe to say you were taught to make sense of what you do not know by logically connecting it to what you already know. That works when information flows in a linear sequence built upon your current knowledge base. However, when it comes to things you did not know, that logic will take you down a dead end, especially if you are unaware of your lack of knowledge in a particular subject. It will look as though the new information or experience is flawed. If you attempt to make it fit nicely into what you have already learned or experienced, you will most likely miss new possibilities in relationships of any kind.

Therefore, I ask that you read through the entire book with an open mind. Be prepared to face thoughts you may not have considered. Also, be prepared to rediscover ideals about relationships that you believe you answered years ago. Before you judge, keep reading. You may find these brilliant ladies have asked the same questions you have, and I answered them. At the same time, if you are left with questions that were not addressed, I encourage you to send me your questions. I would love to hear them.

The Interview Begins

I have the privilege of knowing quite a few brilliant people. Through conversations with them, I can express some of my most complicated and important thoughts.

As the conversation about relationships progressed, the five women had spoken about what they like and do not like about relationships. I, on the other hand, had not expressed anything about my relationship expectations. One of the ladies noticed. She asked me what I wanted from a woman. After my initial answer, she thought the conversation was worthy of sharing with others who struggle to make relationships work. I agreed and thought it would be a good idea to tease more out of the conversation.

The names have been changed to protect the identity of everyone in the room, at their request. I enter the conversation with a simple statement.

"In an intimate relationship, a woman should just give a man what he wants. If she gives him what he wants, the relationship will most likely work," I said.

"So, relationships are just for a man's personal pleasure? What about the woman? Is she entitled to get what she wants?" Susan asked.

"The same applies. The man should just give her what she wants," I replied.

Susan leaned in to hear more as I continued.

"That works if people tell one another what they want up front. That means you talk about what you expect and want from a relationship. If a woman tells me what she wants up front, I can let her know if I can give it to her. If I can't, I'd rather say that up front, instead of her getting upset because she is not getting what she needs. If she lets me know, I can say 'no,

I can't give that to you.' Or I can say 'I'm not willing to give you that.' If I can give it to her, I'll know what I'm getting myself into, instead of her being resentful because she believes she is fulfilling my needs and hers are not being met."

"That sounds like common sense. People should talk about their wants and needs all the time," Susan said.

"Because it does not always happen, I'm not sure if it is common sense. As a man, I've seen something different. A lot of women have a belief that a man is supposed to magically know what she wants. She equates his caring for knowing what she wants without her ever having to tell him anything. I've heard women say that it's a man's job to know, and she should not have to tell him anything. If he doesn't know, he is not really into her. Or he's not paying attention to her. That's not a relationship. That's a babysitting job."

As I finished speaking, the remaining women had become engrossed by my comment. I noticed five pair of eyes watching me as I spoke candidly about a seemingly exhausted topic.

"At the same time, I've also seen women say they only want sex from a man. After they get to know the guy, they like him. Then they claim the rules have changed because feelings are involved. That can be messy," I said. "It's better if you don't judge the person as only being worthy of sex. When you do that, you present yourself as shallow. Later when you change your mind, the person may still see you as shallow. Presenting yourself as shallow is a way of selling yourself short. In addition, it also shows you have poor judgment. People with poor judgment are not always suitable mates."

The silence in the room intensified as I continued giving them more of what they asked for. A couple of the ladies nodded, perhaps in agreement, perhaps in understanding. Nevertheless, as the only man, I had captivated their attention.

"While I understand most people don't know what they want, it's more powerful to say you don't know up front.

Instead, I've seen women not know what they want. Yet, they pretend they do. That can be draining because she is playing trial and error while walking in the dark. If you tell me you don't know what you want, I may still be interested in you. I will know to be patient. However, almost no one has no idea what he or she wants. They may be afraid to ask for it because they don't believe they will get it. That's a little manipulative," I concluded, taking a sip from my glass.

"Sounds like you have a lot of answers. Do you know what you want from a woman?" Susan, the hostess of the gathering, had taken the lead with questions.

"In the simplest way to express what I want, I would say three words: love, affection, and acknowledgement. I'll tell you what I mean by each of those words."

Acknowledgement

"By acknowledgement, I am saying I want to be acknowledged first as a human being. One way to acknowledge me as such is to honor me for having an intelligent contribution. That requires having conversations with me. Talk to me about who you are and what you want from life. Also, it requires listening. That means you listen to what I have to say without interrupting me because you believe what you have to say is more important than what I'm saying." I had given previous thought to this question, so it did not take much for me to answer.

"Furthermore, it requires acknowledgement of my ambitions. If you don't understand them, do not dismiss them. Ask questions. Whether it's career, personal, or a hobby, do not rely on outsiders to advise you on my intentions. Come to me and talk it through. If you don't like what I say, tell me why. Before you become upset, listen to where I'm coming from. Just because you don't like or understand what I say, does not justify being angry or dismissive. Learn to acknowledge my intelligence and understand how I think. An outsider cannot help you with that. Going to someone else, instead of talking it through with me, is a way of not acknowledging me."

My thoughts flowed freely and became audible to those willing to listen.

"As a sidenote, one of the greatest destroyers of love relationships is third party interference. That's from the friend or family member who may or may not have good intentions. Nevertheless, if they give bad advice, they can ruin your relationship. Instead of saying they were wrong, they may fan the flames of misunderstanding between you and your significant other. Then they will say 'I told you so.' That may strictly be the result of the mindset they have. For them, relationships never work. When they see yours working, they may be envious. Or they feel invalidated by you making a relationship work. To save face, they will make suggestions that validate their point of view—relationships don't work.

"Back to acknowledgement, it also means acknowledging my presence in your life by spending time with me. That would include doing new things together. That would allow us to grow together when we share new experiences. It also increases intimacy.

"I would also want a woman who acknowledges the intimacy in me. Acknowledge intimate needs I have. More importantly, I would need her to acknowledge her own intimacy and share it with me. This does not necessarily imply sex.

"While there are thousands of books about relationships, I really don't care what the book says. Acknowledge me as an individual man with individual needs. Regardless of what books say or your experience with other men, I need you to listen to me. If you are always expecting me to do as other men do, you will not be present to me. You will be acknowledging that all men are the same. And that would give you a one size fits all mentality. I have no interest in that. In terms of acknowledgement, anything I say I want, I will offer the same," I had completed my explanation.

"That was quite an explanation, Ted. Care to elaborate on what you mean when you say that you want affection? What exactly does that mean to you?" Susan encouraged me to continue. She scanned the room asking, "We want to hear more ladies? Would you agree?"

"Yes, we want to hear more. This is intriguing!" Tasha said.

"I definitely agree with Tasha. You can't leave us in suspense," Kelly chuckled softly, crossing her legs as she shifted her weight in the chair.

"I'm curious and would love to hear more of what Ted has to say," Andrea added.

Susan looked over at Leslie and waited for her to add to the urging inspired by the other ladies. "Leslie, what do you think? Should Ted go on? Or, shall we silence him now. I think Andrea might want him to stop, but is too polite to say so," Susan teased, as Andrea laughed and shook her head in disagreement.

A smile warmed Leslie's face, as she uncrossed her arms, allowing them to rest on the arms of the chair.

"Well," Susan said, "Ted and I have had similar conversations before, so some of these things I have heard before, while other thoughts are new to me."

"I know you ladies are not going to allow him to leave without further explanation, so I say, carry on, Ted."

Leslie laughed as she leaned back in her chair taking a sip from her glass. I laughed too, appreciating their levity.

Affection

The twilight moon peered over the Manhattan cityscape as I proceeded to offer the ladies insight into my thoughts about relationships. I had found myself in a situation that did not happen very often. Offering my more in-depth thoughts to a group of women was not a new experience, but it had been a while. I had done so with individuals, maybe at times in a group with other men, but this was a rare opportunity. Perhaps, the wine had lowered inhibitions, offering more pliable ears to hear what I was saying. Regardless of the reasons, I was eager to continue.

"When I say affection, I am not necessarily talking about sex. However, affection during sex is important. By affection, I am talking about touch. Touching is very important to me. It also refers to a woman's voice; the way she speaks. Affection also includes the way a woman listens. There isn't much affection in judgment. Affectionate listening has a certain kind of openness and kindness. It also allows for freedom in the way I express myself to her.

"Affection is not limited to foreplay. It is something that occurs throughout the day no matter where we are. In other words, sex and affection happens way before you get to the bedroom.

"Affection seems to have lost its importance in relationships. Women now talk about being tough and independent. I am clueless as to how tough and independent is relevant in a love relationship. Nor do I understand the idea of having my back. The only time I would need a woman to be tough or have my back is if we are going to prison together."

I heard the chuckles of the women as I went on with my explanation.

"In prison, there will likely be physical threats. Being tough would be relevant. For that matter, so would having my back. Otherwise, there is nothing I can do with toughness. I can't #$%@ it. I can't deposit it in the bank. I can't buy anything with it. I can't barter with it. It has no value in a relationship unless you are in environments that present physical threats. What kind of man is going to take you places where your physical and emotional well-being can be jeopardized? Toughness brings no value to my life," I completed my thought.

"Believe it or not it is possible to remain affectionate with your significant other even in the face of a disagreement. Disagreements do not mean there is something wrong with the relationship. It only requires acknowledging the other person's thought process, which requires an affectionate listening," I added.

"Hmmm, affectionate listening," Tasha said. "I've never heard that term before. That's deep to me."

"If you watch new relationships Tasha, that kind of affection exists. For some reason, however, people believe it is no longer necessary once you know the person. When I list love, affection, and acknowledgement, I mention them as building blocks to maintain a great relationship. Those building blocks will always be part of the relationship," I explained.

"I hear you, Ted. Like Tasha, I've never heard that term before, but what exactly does that look like? I've heard of active listening but not affectionate listening," Andrea admitted.

"For me," I said, "I love to touch a woman. I'll touch her anytime. For one, it's a way to show affection and appreciation for her. Secondly, it is a way to acknowledge her presence. Third, it's one way to build deep intimacy.

"With that said, since I love touching my woman, I want to touch a body that feels pleasant to my hands. That means she needs to take care of her body. I have no interest in touching a woman whose body is overweight. If she is unwilling to take care of the only body she will ever have, why would I fool myself to believe she would consistently take care of me? If you don't care about yourself, why should I?

"Besides, when a person is overweight, that extra weight puts unnecessary stress on internal organs. That impedes the effectiveness of those internal organs and restricts blood flow. Restricted blood flow affects brain function. Without optimal blood flow, the brain is less effective. A less effective brain affects decision-making and can easily contribute to poor decision-making. Poor decision-making causes frustration, and the person could do anything from ineffective communication to eating unhealthy foods. That exacerbates frustration and poor decision-making. As you see, the cycle continues. It's an endless trap. Being overweight leads to illnesses. In many cases, it's a premature death for the overweight person," I said.

"Now this is an interesting shift in the conversation," Kelly stated.

"How so, Kelly? Do you find my mention of a woman's weight offensive?" I asked.

"No," she replied, "it's just that I've never heard a man explain it like you are. I understand, however, why you might ask if I think it's offensive. Weight can be a touchy subject with women."

"So, a healthy body is not only pleasant to the touch, it also supports healthy dynamics in a relationship," I continued. "Besides, once you gain weight, you are no longer the same person. People will not treat you the same. The way people treat you affects how you see yourself. How you see yourself has everything to do with who you are."

"Hmmm, another deep consideration," Tasha said.

Love

"When it comes to love, that is much more complex," I said, as Leslie and Tasha nodded in agreement.

"That is an understatement, Ted," Susan laughed.

"People have an image of love based on Hollywood, books, and the media. That's not love. It's an image. Images are not the thing you claim you want. That's like being in a relationship with a picture of someone. The picture is an image. You can have all kinds of fantasies about the person in the picture. However, there will be no shared responsibility. It takes two for love, if love is the right word to use."

"What do you mean, if love is the right word to use?" Andrea asked.

"Most people fall in love with ideas about love," I said. "It almost has nothing to do with the person they claim to love. I've even heard women say they are happy to be in love with love. The R&B group the Spinners had a song called, *It takes a fool to learn that love don't love no one*. Loving love is the same as loving the picture of a person. Love does not love you back. Loving love is like having a love relationship with air. Just because air is there for you doesn't mean it is in love with you. It's just there."

"In fact," I continued, "you don't need a person or object of your desire to be in love with love. You can simply sit in a room and make the claim you are having a love affair with love. What you learn is love doesn't even acknowledge you. While you are sitting in your room alone, you will find that love does not touch you or provide any physical affection or intimacy. You will be alone. Even though it doesn't mean you are lonely, you will be by yourself having fantasies about what love will do for you. The reality is as you sit in your room alone love will be doing nothing for you. Being in a love relationship requires responsibility on both parties. That means you both take actions. At the same time, perhaps love has nothing to do with actions. Maybe the most powerful form of love occurs by two people being able to experience 'being' with one another. Just being with someone without words or touching is a great way to experience intimacy.

"By doing so, one of the things you may learn is love is a creative act. It has nothing to do with gifts or Hollywood. I would say the greatest gift anyone can give is to give themselves. That has nothing to do with the amount of time you spend together. That means vulnerability and trust. That would have you experience the person without presuppositions based on what you've heard about other men from books or experience. That woman would experience me for who I am with her. With her, I may be a man I've never been with anyone. Many women miss this because of the fairy tales they've been sold about the prince in shining armor. And they never learn what kind of woman they have to be to attract that prince. That's irresponsible. I'm interested in a woman who wants to get to know me and give herself to me. I may not have interest in living out the script of the prince, especially if she does not know the role of the princess. If she has not been properly educated as a princess, she is asking me to participate in a farce, inauthentic relationship. Besides, I'd much rather get to know her for who she is."

There was dead silence in the room as I talked at length sharing my thoughts which represented a myriad of previous conversations with various people. Fortunately, the silence was not uncomfortable. Quite the opposite. I felt compelled by the silence of these bright women to continue, so I did.

Did You Sign the Contract?

"I often tell people that I never signed that contract," I said.

"Okay, now I'm lost," Kelly interjected. I anticipated some puzzlement by my statement; nevertheless, once again those previous conversations about love and relationships came flooding back to my memory. I was equipped with an explanation.

"It appears when men and women meet, they are following a script. I have said that when I was in the hospital the day of my birth, they presented me with several contracts and scripts. They told me all I had to do was put my footprint on the dotted line, and I would have signed the contract. Because I refused to sign it, I don't really know the content. I don't know the lines in the script that it appears most are following. And I don't have interest in knowing the lines in the script. Therefore, I am under no obligation to follow any script," I paused to take a drink.

Susan, being the hospitable woman that she was, politely re-filled my glass as I continued.

"While I know that can be challenging for many women, it requires her to step up and be herself. And that can be confusing if she has been following the script all her life. I would be taking her into uncharted territory. From what I've seen, most women are uncomfortable with that notion. Yet, it's so freeing to experience yourself without the script. Freedom is one thing I will offer a woman.

"I hear most women say they are already free. Except, they are following a script. And they want me or another guy to go along with the script she is reading from. I've always found that wild. So many women say they want a man who is not like other men. As soon as they meet that guy, they expect him to do what she has seen other guys do. If he doesn't, she becomes uncomfortable and backs off. Because she does not recognize what he's doing, she believes he's playing a game. As a result, she attempts to manipulate him onto the script she was given. As you can imagine, that doesn't last long, especially for the guy who has his head together. However, if she is physically attractive, the guy may stay around for a short while and follow the script. Unfortunately, she will not be taken seriously. When he gets tired of the relationship (script) and leaves, she will feel she was used for sex. Men with high intelligence are rarely interested in following the same script you use with all men. In some ways, that's an insult," I sighed. "That's all I have to say about this topic ladies," I stood up to stretch.

"Wow! I should have recorded this conversation. That sounds like a book," Kelly said.

"Hhhmmm. Okay," was my only reply.

"I didn't expect you to be so clear about what you want. With so many people struggling to build relationships, everything you said could help. As you already know, people are having a difficult time building relationships. What you laid out would help so many people," Susan said.

"To me, it appears relationships have changed. I met a woman in 1991. She and I lived together for five years. In 1996, I left the country and did not return until 1999. From the time I lived with this woman until I returned to the US, it appears something happened. Whatever it was that happened, I was not part of it. I was either living with someone or out of the country," I said.

"There appears to be more fear in people, especially when it comes to love. There is so much anger and fear that people cannot even share love. In New York, they claim to be cynical. Cynicism is a form of fear disguised as caution. New Yorkers are afraid of 'hello.' I have no idea what happened to people.

"If I guess, it may have something to do with the battle of the sexes. There is no reason to ever have a battle of the sexes. It is unnatural for the sexes to battle. There is nothing in nature that displays the sexes fight with one another. Nature designed the sexes, so they need one another. We seem to believe we can defy nature. Every time you defy nature, you pay a price. Perhaps because we are working against nature, we are paying a price. Now people cannot find love. They have replaced love with anger and fear. The result is loneliness. That is the cost of defying nature," I said.

Shaking her head in agreement, Tasha said, "That's true. People never win when they defy nature."

"How can relationships ever work if one person spends time invalidating the other? While I know people only do what they were taught to do, at some point, someone has to wake up and see the current behavior isn't working and it never worked. It's time to end the battle of the sexes and get clear about what you offer. Most people focus on what they expect from the other. In many cases, they expect more than what they offer. If you can't give what you want, do you really have the right to ask for it?"

"I notice you talk about 'I' a lot. You don't seem like a selfish man, but, from what you're saying now, you sound like you only focus on yourself," Andrea said.

"Of course, there are lots of 'I' and 'me' comments, You asked what 'I' want from a woman. When you ask any man or me that question there is no 'we.' I'm Ted Santos, and I'm a unique individual with unique needs. Likely, you don't know what those needs are, until I tell you what they are. When I say what I want, I don't care what you want. We are talking about *me*. I just need you to hear and acknowledge what I say. Then let me know if you can give me what I need. If not, let me know up front," I answered, looking directly at Andrea.

"Okay," she did not break eye contact. "I can see that," she continued, "it's a little intense. But, it forces one to refocus on the individual, not the 'we.'"

"It's a partnership. You need to understand what I'm capable of contributing. You also need to understand what is required from a woman to keep me engaged in a monogamous relationship." I had broken eye contact with Andrea to observe the other women in the room. I agreed with Andrea; my comment was intense. I think the other women agreed, too.

"If I have to express my needs in terms of 'we,' I am no longer being acknowledged. Ted Santos as an individual has disappeared. That could easily set up the mindset of compromise," I said.

"If you understand negotiation, you may not have to compromise. The key to negotiation is to understand what the other person wants. If you understand that, you may be able to offer the same thing in a different form. With that approach, no one has to give up anything. Compromise often creates resentment, especially if one person believes they compromise the most. Or it can become a tool for manipulation. One person will remind you they compromised the last couple of times. Now it's your turn.

"Negotiation is not just for business. If you learn to effectively negotiate with your significant other, you will have that skill for other aspects of your life. From another perspective, and as a man, there are many women who do not listen to what a man says. If 'I,' as a man, say I don't like something, there are women who will tell me that I will learn to like it. That is a way of not acknowledging me as a human being. The same applies when you claim I should stop talking about the needs of 'I' or 'me.' When you tell a person, they should not talk about 'I' or 'me,' you have, in some ways, invalidated their needs. This is the prevailing mindset that promotes sacrifice and compromise."

Finishing, I noticed what appeared to be shock on a few faces. Tasha appeared to be in deep thought, while Kelly looked as though she wasn't sure if she agreed or disagreed. The women sat quietly. I interpreted their quietness as a signal to go on with what I had to say.

"When I was twenty-seven, I realized that an average woman would never be able to have a fulfilling relationship with me. I've always looked for a woman who could bring something extraordinary to the relationship. Because those women are rare, at twenty-seven, I came up with a way to communicate to women who may have been following a script.

"Imagine that every man comes in packaging. Maybe all the men you dated came wrapped in the red package. Perhaps your father and brother were also wrapped in the red package. Therefore, you know the red package, and you are comfortable with it. You know what to expect from it. And when you consider a man for a relationship, you look for the guy in the red package.

"I, on the other hand, may be in the blue package. Since you have no experience with the blue package, I suggest you take your time and get to know the contents of the blue. If you expect the blue to give you everything in the red, you may miss out on the uniqueness of the blue. If you unwrapped the blue package, you may find everything you like about the red plus things you never experienced from guys in the red package.

"And if you look close, I may be a color package you've never seen before. I may have nothing in common with the guys in red, blue, green, or orange packaging. They may all be following scripts that are part of the color packaging they were given. I ask you to be open-minded and explore the kind of man I am. You will find I'm wrapped in no packaging. With me, you will no longer have to be confined to the packaging or script they gave you. There is another world outside of the scripts they handed to everyone. You will be able to experience yourself in a way you may never have in the past.

"Getting to know me is a way to get to know yourself in a way you may not have ever considered. That may be one of the most powerful expressions of love," I said.

"Ted, people always want to make a great first impression. It's a delicate balance to talk about yourself without saying too much," Leslie said.

"I once heard someone jokingly say that when you first meet someone, they send their representative. The real person does not show up for several months to a year," I said.

"I honestly do not think it takes that long for the true representative to show up. Ladies, would you agree?" Leslie looked around the room for confirmation. The other women nodded offering short audible affirmations, indicating that Leslie's comment was a general consensus.

"If that is considered making a good first impression, it is deceitful," I said. "I'd rather know who you are up front. I think I'm smart enough to know what I want. If you attempt to show me what you think I want, it could backfire," I completed my thought.

Pausing, to take another sip from my drink, I added more to my previous statement.

"From where I stand," I continued, "all human beings have a story. Therefore, at some point, we can all relate to one another. If you spend any time with a person, you learn their story and how they became who they are. From what I've seen, everyone has many stories. At some point, the person tells a story that makes you bond. If you force a good impression, you can miss that bonding opportunity. You don't always know what makes people bond. So, it's best to be naturally yourself. The funny thing is even if people don't initially like one another, there still may be a story that makes them bond and see one another in a different light," I said.

"Okay. I see what you are doing. You first talked about what you want specifically. Then you talk about how you and a woman make things work together," Andrea quickly responded.

"Technically, I am always speaking in terms of 'we and us.' I simply point out that the individual is responsible for the relationship. It doesn't work on its own.

"In some ways, I see a relationship between two people as the creation of a third. When two people come together, they make a third person. The third person is an amalgamation of the two. And the third person has to be taken care of by both. If one abandons the job of caring for the third, there is a good chance the relationship will die."

I surveyed the room. Although Susan initiated many questions, the other women had begun to pose their own questions, allowing me to dig deeper and reveal my thoughts on the matter at hand. Silence blanketed the room.

"You said something earlier about sex," Tasha spoke up, breaking the momentary silence. "There are women who attempt to be like guys. They tell men they only want sex. As a woman, I couldn't do that. I'm very emotional. So, I don't like hooking up with a lot of different men. Even for the women who think they can just 'hook up,' most eventually become emotionally attached. So, I can see how that would be messy. It seems to take men longer to get emotionally attached."

"I think women should be comfortable being the way you are. While I know that I can't speak for all men, I can say with confidence that men love the fact women can bond. However, like women, we don't want to be possessed or obligated just because we shared sexual intimacy," I said.

"Really?" Tasha said. "That's insightful."

"With that said, in no way am I promoting promiscuity," I continued," I am saying two things. First, I will discuss something that is somewhat technical. Men and women's brains do not function the same. While everyone has naturally occurring chemicals in the brain, the chemicals or neurochemicals are not equal between men and women."

Andrea crossed her legs and leaned back in her chair. "They are not equal?" she said. "That suggests to me that one may be superior to another, Ted."

"There is a neurochemical called oxytocin," I paused. "You ladies are familiar with that?" I asked.

A euphony of agreement encouraged me to continue. "It is called the bonding or love chemical. The brains of men and women secrete oxytocin. Except, women's brains secrete significantly more than men. When a woman is pregnant and breastfeeding, her oxytocin levels are extremely high. That is why you see women bond with babies so easily. Nature made it that way."

"Also," I said, "during sexual intercourse, oxytocin levels increase for men and women. The woman's brain simply secretes more than the man's. And that is what contributes to a woman's loving and affectionate nature. As men, we love that. When we don't get it, it can be frustrating. Because men do not secrete as much oxytocin, many women believe we are withholding or playing it cool. It's not that we are withholding; it just takes longer for bonding to take place in us. In fact, testosterone blocks oxytocin. So, if a woman argues with a man often, his brain may likely secrete testosterone. And bonding becomes more difficult."

"Now that is insightful information!" Kelly said. "Testosterone blocks oxytocin? Wow!"

"It seems nature gave women the responsibility of creating bonds in relationships. We call women nurturers. If women took ownership of that, perhaps relationships would have a higher success rate. If a woman is depending on a man to be responsible for bonding, it will most likely take longer," I said.

"That makes sense," was Kelly's only remark.

"The second thing I am saying about sex and bonding is that it is not in a woman's best interest to believe all men want one thing—sex. It would be in societies best interest to stop spreading that myth. All men need more than sex," I added. "As men, we are taught that we must provide more than sex to a woman. We are to make her feel physically, emotionally, and financially safe. Some women like gifts—flowers, jewelry, etc. Or they expect a man to treat her to dinner, vacations, outings, etc. Those are things a man is responsible for if he wants the relationship to work long term. Moreover, we are taught that and other things from the time we were little boys."

If, on the other hand, women are taught that men only want sex, she will miss out on providing a man with the things he needs to sustain a long-term relationship. There is a good chance that a man can walk away from a woman, even after good sex, because he does not believe his other needs will be met. It's difficult to commit to someone who does not appear to care about your other needs. While sex creates a great bond, men need more than that for a lasting bond. It takes the effort of two to make a relationship work."

"Wait, Ted! I understand when you say women expect men to 'just know' what she wants. I used to do that. But I learned how much easier it is when you communicate your needs. The problem comes when you have been in a few relationships that have failed. When you had relationships with men who were not good communicators. Then you become a little confused because the next man wants something completely different. How should we, as women, learn from our past mistakes?" Susan asked.

"That's a good question. You may not like my answer," I said. "So, I'll start with questions. If you ran a $1 billion company and you needed a CPA to help with your finances and corporate taxes, would you hire someone who didn't even have experience or a degree in accounting?"

"Of course not. That wouldn't even make sense. What does a CPA have to do with my question?" Susan asked.

"I know," I said, looking around the room. I had the women's attention, so I finished my answer to Susan. "It seems like an irrelevant question. Stay with me," I encouraged. " Why wouldn't you hire someone without any accounting experience or degree?"

"Again, common sense says they will mess up my finances. With a $1 billion company, I can't afford to have someone playing trial and error with my books," she replied.

"Exactly! Furthermore, a good CPA will be able to provide you with a financial perspective on long-term strategy." Saying that, I knew they understood my point.

"Okay. Sure. So, what?" Susan asked.

"It's interesting that we are trained to put more effort and diligence into a company than we put into our own lives. Why wouldn't you or anyone else put the same thinking into creating a long-term love relationship?" I continued with my example, "If you won't hire someone without accounting or CPA experience, why hire someone in your life who has no experience with relationships? Just because you have had relationships does not mean you know what you are doing. The problem is there is nowhere for us to go to get the proper training to have a great relationship. We end up playing trial and error in the lives of others. What's most troubling is many people have no idea what they offer the other person. Combine that with the fact they have no clue about what they want in the relationship and you have a disaster in the making. If you need a CPA, you don't hire an engineer to do the job. Most people hire the wrong person in their love life and then complain about them. When you hire a CPA, you hire them because you know exactly what you need from them. If they offer more than a CPA, that's a bonus," I said.

"At the same time, you wouldn't hire a highly qualified CPA to do your corporate taxes if you have no company or no plans to create a company. Even if you paid that CPA a great salary, they would be sitting around bored doing nothing daily. In the end, both of you will be frustrated. That is an example of what I mean by having something to offer the other. In either case, it requires that men and women develop themselves. The kind of development to which I am referring does not come from a formal education. It requires you to take the time to learn about yourself and who you are. That makes it easier to know what you want. To do that requires more than a self-help book. There are lots of transformational workshops that help you discover yourself. If you have not seriously invested in yourself at that level, you are playing trial and error in another person's life. And most likely you have learned more about what you don't want instead of what you do want."

"You're a little different than most guys," Kelly was the first to respond. "For one, you have your own interesting diet—vegetarian—and you work out a lot. You're well traveled, and you read a lot of stuff. It seems like you develop yourself mentally, physically, and spiritually. Your approach to life is holistic. Will you help a woman take the same holistic approach to life? Will you help her be a better woman?"

"Hhhhmmmm, I never thought of it as holistic," I paused for a moment to consider the thought. I went on, "I can see why someone would say that. However, what I'm really talking about is being responsible. You get one body and mind. You are the only one responsible for taking care of it. If you won't take care of your body and mind, how can I expect that you will take care of a growing, thriving relationship?"

"So, you are only interested in taking care of yourself?" Kelly asked.

"If you do take care of yourself, then I would look forward to making you a better woman. And because you are the most important person in my life, I would look forward to you making me a better man," was my answer.

"Okay. I'm with you on that," Kelly said in agreement.

"A relationship seems like it is the best place to grow. Like I said already, two people make a third. That third person is a combination of the two of you. While I take care of that third person, I learn from it. I learn from what you feed into it, just as you learn from what I feed into it. That kind of relationship makes you extremely important to one another. You are so important to one another that you affect every aspect of one another's lives. I can't think of someone who is more important.

"A woman like that affects my career, the way I raise children, the way I relate to friends and family. She will also affect hobbies, vacations and new experiences.

"I hear people talk about souls. However, I've never seen one. So, I focus on what I do know and what I can affect. That would be speaking, listening, seeing, touching and moving," I said.

"This is my first time meeting you. I've heard your name before. You do talk differently than most men. You're very unique," Leslie commented.

"Thank you. Perhaps it's fair to say we are all unique, and we have creative ways of expressing it," I said.

"Talk about being unique. Can we go back to something you said earlier? You gave a unique perspective on being tough and independent. Some men are not reliable. So, we, as women, must be tough when a man leaves and independent so we can make it on our own. You make it sound like being tough and independent can hurt a woman's chances of being with a great guy," Susan asked.

"As I said before, being tough has no intrinsic value. If two people in a relationship make a third, what purpose does being tough serve? Tough implies anger. Anger can make you miss opportunities. I would prefer someone who is honest with her communication and firm with her word. In other words, she keeps her word. A person can be tough and never keep their word. Being firm can establish boundaries without alienating others. Alienating others can cost you more than you earn. It's very difficult to get 'we' if you are in the habit of alienating people. That goes for personal and professional life. Tough is usually a sign of fear," I said.

"As for making a woman feel safe, my response may be tricky. I can't make anyone feel anything. Everyone is responsible for what they feel. Therefore, I can't make a woman feel safe. I do understand a woman seeks a level of physical, emotional, and financial security. There are many women who choose big muscular men for the comfort of physical safety, while others seek men who are affluent for financial safety. If you, as a woman, feel unsafe, that unsafe feeling is what you bring to a relationship. Technically speaking, you need to get that handled. Otherwise, you may be expecting me to change you. Besides, if we are creating a third person together, you will be feeding the feeling of not being safe into it.

"With that said, the feeling of love, happiness, safety, courage, etc. are the individual's responsibility to bring to the relationship. I can't give them to you. As a side, in many cases, toughness is a substitute when the others are missing," I said, finishing my thought.

"From what you just said, it sounds like you go into relationships like a business," Susan said. "Some women may see you as a tough, no nonsense guy. You say you are not responsible for making her happy. While I understand what you are saying, it may be difficult for other women to understand that. Perhaps that understanding comes with being more seasoned in life."

She continued, "I guess what I'm saying is there have been so many parts of this conversation that make you sound like a guy who is deeply in love with a wonderful woman. Then you come along and make a somewhat stern remark like 'I'm not responsible for your happiness.' Now you suddenly don't sound like this loving and affectionate guy you presented in the beginning."

"I can see that," I said. "There are probably many women who see me that way."

"That's it! That's all you have to say?" Susan, disappointed by what I said, went on to express her let down.

"You always seem so self-expressed. Now you're saying, 'So what? The end?'"

Tasha stood up, straightened her skirt, and said, "I need another drink."

As the cacophony of disappointment ensued, Andrea joined her.

I laughed. Their abrupt responses caught me off guard.

I went on, "No. A friend of mine was married to this beautiful South American woman. I once asked his wife about her opinion of me. I said that many women might see me as having some physical attractiveness. However, there may be something about me that makes women cautious of me or even turn them off. What do you think that could be?

"She said, 'You look like a guy who doesn't play games. You look like you don't take $#%@ from anyone.' I said, 'Well I thought women liked guys who don't play games.' She said, 'True, but every woman has her own stuff. You look like you just won't allow or accept it. So, a woman would leave you alone, regardless of how you look.'"

Refreshed drink in hand, Tasha made her way back to her seat.

Andrea remained standing, quietly talking on her phone.

"I can see why she said that," Tasha said taking her seat. "You don't mind women seeing you that way?" she asked.

"It has nothing to do with what I mind or don't mind," I said. "I mentioned earlier about men coming in red, blue, or green packaging. From what you and the South American woman are saying, you have a presupposition about what a man is or how he is supposed to be. Without knowing it, you are expecting a one-size-fits-all. Or you expect me to read from the script. As I said, I never signed the contract to follow the script."

"Are you being a smart ass now?" Andrea had returned to her seat, looking uncertain.

"No," I said. "I'm simply saying that I'm all the things I've said. You can't know what I offer until you get to know me. If a woman enjoys playing games as part of getting to know a guy, I am most likely not the guy for her. You see, I understand that whatever it takes to get a person is what it takes to keep them. Or however the relationship starts is what you can expect throughout. If it starts with games, there will be games throughout the entire relationship. The fact a person believes playing games is natural says something about their mindset. It could be saying they have no idea how to create a relationship that is designed to build something with a person. So, they play games to have excitement. They believe that excitement will create a bond. The game does not make me a better man. For me, it is a waste of brain cells to have to figure out what game you are playing today. Instead of playing games, focus on developing yourself so you are happy, intelligent, emotionally safe, etc. That way it won't be my job to make you feel those things. I'll do the same for myself. Then we can focus on what we are building together."

"That makes sense. I guess like you said earlier, a woman would have to unwrap your packaging," Tasha said, leaning forward to sit her drink on the table in front of her.

"It's better when she sees I don't come in any packaging to unwrap," I said.

"So, what is a woman to do with you in the beginning? Does she interview you like in a job? That doesn't sound like fun," Kelly's questions seemed to echo the thoughts of the other women.

"I've had women say they felt like they were on a job interview with me. I've also seen women do the same. Those women knew exactly what they wanted. They were playing no games with their lives. Women who know what they want are usually up front and direct. When a woman is like that, it makes the guy wake up. He is either going to be straight with the woman and give her what she wants or leave her alone. Some guys may attempt to play games with her. Except, she won't stick around long.

"At the same time," I continued, "there are many women who play games from day one. They pretend to not be interested when they are. They say they have a boyfriend when they don't. Or they don't tell you they have a boyfriend. For me, the funniest thing is they play the game of chase me, chase me. That way she feels like she is worth something to you. All those games produce zero results. They are demonstrations of what you bring to the table. If you're interested and pretend you're not, you're dishonest. What a way to start things off. The same when you lie about having or not having a boyfriend. As I said earlier, however you start a relationship is what will be part of the relationship throughout. If you start with lies, don't be surprised.

"Furthermore, if you need me to chase you to make you feel good, you and I are not equals. There is a good chance that that kind of woman is insecure and constantly seeking some sort of validation. While I understand many of us have been raised to believe we have issues, it can be draining to be with a woman who plays games to get validation. That is why I say it's important for a woman to bring her own happiness.

"As a sidenote, I once dated an extraordinarily beautiful woman who told me the following: 'I know there are women who are more beautiful than me. There are women who are smarter than me. There are women who have better hair and nails than me. There are women who are better lovers than me. There are women who have better bodies than me. There are women who are better educated than me. However, there is no woman who can offer all those things together better than me. I know I offer all those things. So, I don't worry about competition from other women.'"

"I like that!" Tasha said. "Her confidence is impressive. I want that kind of confidence!" Tasha fluffed the pillow in her chair, picked up her drink, and leaned in to hear more.

"Exactly, Tasha," I said. "I was stunned by that conversation. It explained a lot about her. She did carry herself with that kind of solid confidence. It also explained why she didn't expect me to tell her how beautiful she was. As gorgeous as she was, she only asked me once why I didn't tell her she was beautiful. I asked her if she needed that. She said 'no'. Then I told her I thought she was unbelievably gorgeous. And for the next fifteen minutes we complimented one another.

"Instead of spending all our time complimenting one another on looks, she and I spent more time building one another up," I continued, "With her, I felt more invincible than ever. Unfortunately, life pulled us in many different directions, especially when I lost both my parents. Later she died of lupus."

"Oh, my!" Leslie exclaimed. "Sorry to hear that. So, you lost three important people in your life?"

"I guess I did. I never thought of it that way."

A reverent hush fell over the room, as I began to further explain.

"I brought her up because she gave me what I wanted. And she knew me for being loving and affectionate, even though I wasn't saying all the sweet things a man is 'supposed' to say. I had an extraordinarily intimate relationship with her, even after not seeing her for years. In some ways, our relationship never died."

Leslie looked up from her glass, "Okay. I appreciate that," was her only reply.

The atmosphere was somber. The fire burning in the fireplace once welcomed us into this lavish room, warding off the fall Manhattan chill. Now, it failed to remove the chill of me sharing a memory of my departed loved one. There was more I wanted to share, so I went on, unsure of how my next statement would be received.

"There is something else," I continued, as the women sat and looked. Their silence was an invite for me to go on with my thought.

Almost in unison, each woman echoed the others question, "What is that?"

"In life, if you ask a person what they stand for, they may have nothing to say. Or they will tell you what they think they are supposed to say, like contributing or world peace. World peace requires you to travel around the world to make peace with people who have conflict. If you're not doing that, you are not really standing for world peace. And giving to an organization is an irresponsible way to express your contribution. Giving money takes you off the hook from being responsible for anything.

"With that said, if most people are unable to tell you what they stand for, there is a good chance they are not standing for their significant other. Perhaps that is what people are attempting to communicate when they say, 'I have your back.' You can't really build anything out of having your back. Having your back is more defensive.

"Standing for someone, on the other hand, is a creative act that allows you to build. When you stand for someone, you are committed to him or her as their commitments. In fact, you won't even allow them to be less than you know they are. If your significant other is not getting what they want in life, you will brainstorm with them to create solutions. Or you will make resources available to support them. Resources include intellectual capital, contacts, money, etc. And you are advocating for them when they are not around. At the same time, it does not mean you have to do the same things they are doing to be supportive. You support them as they pursue their individual commitments. Ultimately, you become a stand for them. In other words, you become a platform for them to create what they want in life. That surely requires they are leaving your presence in a much better mindset daily. That does not mean faking. It's just that you know their success in life is affected by their relationship with you," I said.

Andrea tilted her head and fixed her eyes on me as I continued to speak.

"So," I said, "the woman I mentioned above is someone I stood for. Some would say I believed in her. I suggested she pursue things because I knew she had what it took to be successful. And I was there to understand the challenges and help her work through them. I wanted her to get what she wanted in life, whether it was from career, family, friends or me. I stood for her being a powerful and successful woman, who just happened to be beautiful. If I bring it all together, if you are playing games in a relationship, it's very difficult to stand for one another. Playing games can tarnish trust and breed resentment. When you powerfully stand for one another, you can kill trust.

"That sounds deep. What do you mean kill trust? Everyone knows trust is an important element in any relationship," Tasha asked.

"Yes, for most, it's common sense to depend on trust to create a relationship of any kind. Except, I ask that you consider a couple of things. When you depend on trust in a love relationship, you are depending on something outside of the couple. The most important thing is that trust never travels alone. It never leaves home without its faithful companion," I said.

"What are you talking about, Ted? 'Tasha asked.

"Yeah, I'm with Tasha on that one. What exactly are you saying? You're not making sense," Susan shook her head.

"What I am saying is this, trust always travels with a companion. Do you know who that companion is?" I asked.

"No. I'm sure you'll tell me though," Tasha replied.

"Yes, I will," I smiled hoping to create further intrigue. I answered, "First I want you to think about it. When you depend on trust you are depending on something outside of the people involved."

"So," Andrea said, "what else are you supposed to depend on? Are you following him Susan? Because I am lost now? He said, 'kill trust.' Why would anyone do that?"

"I'm with you on that one, Andrea," Susan stated in frustration.

"When you are building a relationship with trust you never factor in that trust has a companion waiting around the corner to jump in and run the show," I went on." While you are sitting there happy because trust is doing a great job, you never see trust's companion lurking in the shadows."

"Okay, Ted," Andrea said, "aren't you getting a little dramatic with this?"

"Well," I said, "who is trust's faithful companion?"

In a demanding cacophony, the women shouted, "Tell us already!"

"The only thing you should kill right now is the suspense!" Susan exclaimed.

"Ted," Leslie asked, "could trust's companion be misunderstanding?"

"You're kind of in the neighborhood," I replied.

"Oh my God!" Kelly said. "We are never going to guess, just tell us. Please."

"Okay. Okay," I said. "Trust's companion is mistrust," I answered.

Kelly lightly tapped her forehead, "Ahhh!" she said. "But why would you kill trust? Are you sure you mean that?"

"Absolutely positively yes," I said. "In fact, you want to take trust in the backyard and shoot it in the head and leave it to die.

"Like I said Kelly, dramatic!" Andrea re-emphasized her point.

"Think about it. Every time you talk about whether you trust someone, mistrust is waiting around the corner for its opportunity to enter the relationship. However, if you kill trust, mistrust dies with it," I said.

"That doesn't make sense, Ted. It takes time to trust someone," Andrea said.

"Yes," I said. "That is what you are taught. At the same time, you are depending on something outside of yourself to create a powerful relationship with another person and the relationship."

Tasha posed another question, "So, what are you using to build the relationship?"

"Your word," my simple answer beckoned for further explanation. "If I kill trust with you, I don't have to think about whether you are lying. If you said you would do something, I know you honor your word as yourself. In other words, your word is your bond. So, if you tell me something, I don't give it another thought. I don't even consider whether you lied or whether I should trust what you say. To me, you are your word.

"That is kind of what it is like to powerfully stand for someone. There is nothing to figure out. Nevertheless, you are always communicating with one another. Nothing magically happens. And you are both responsible for your contribution to one another and the relationship."

"Okay," Kelly said. "When you give your word, the person will feel like they can trust you if you are consistent about it over time."

"That is the paradigm we have been given. We wait for a person to prove themselves over time. When we feel like they are deserving of our trust because they keep their word, we trust them. What I am saying is, kill trust from the beginning," I re-emphasized.

"Sit down," I said, "and have a conversation that says, 'here is how I operate. I would like to kill trust between you and me.'"

"Did you do this with someone?" Andrea asked.

"I have," I answered. "I let her know that if she and I depend on trust, it is something outside of us that is creating the relationship. Furthermore, if we depend on trust, mistrust will be waiting to come in and run the relationship. Mistrust waits for a misunderstanding or disagreement. But, usually mistrust is always trying to step into your relationship and run things. If we kill trust, mistrust will die with it. Without trust or mistrust, we only have our word. If I say I will do something, you already know it is done because I said so. If I'm delayed, I will let you know. The same goes if I say I will meet you somewhere at 5:00 p.m. You don't even have to waste your time wondering if I will be late or playing some kind of game. You know I honor myself as my word. My word is my bond.

"So, Kelly, this is not about how you feel about the person. If you depend on feelings, you are waiting for indicators to let you know if you feel they are trustworthy. I'm saying you can establish that kind of relationship from the beginning."

"And you think people will understand or want to do this?" Andrea asked in disbelief.

"Why do you think people would not?" I asked.

"Because no one thinks this way," Andrea firmly stated nodding her head no. "We are all taught to trust some and not trust others. Here you come with some new paradigm that throws everything we know right out the window." She paused, then continued, "Oh! I forgot. You took trust and mistrust to the backyard and shot them in the head." Andrea pointed her finger in the air, "Boom, boom!!" she exclaimed.

I laughed, "Who's being dramatic now?"

Andrea , drawing her finger back, teased, "You think you're funny."

"It's really not funny," I said. "It says a lot about how people value their own word."

"I don't think it's a matter of valuing your word," Susan said. "It just sounds hard or like a lot of work."

"Why?" I asked.

"It sounds like you have to be perfect," Susan added.

"Exactly!" Andrea shouted.

"Yeah, Ted," Tasha joined in, "you're not allowed to make any mistakes."

I said, "It sounds like that because it is new. New paradigms always sound a little strange or like hard work. It really is a matter of being your word. You see, like I said, if you depend on something outside of your relationship to make it work, you are in trouble. You have to understand that, while trust appears to be on your side, you don't see mistrust is waiting to step in and take over. Once mistrust takes over, your relationship can become turbulent and stressful. Imagine mistrust providing guidance in your relationship. Both trust and mistrust are outside elements. However, when you depend on yourself and your word, that is a very different mindset. It is a much higher commitment. If I say I will do something, I will do it. If I say I will not do it, I don't do it. It really is a matter of integrity. Integrity means whole and complete. Imagine having your word to one another be whole and complete. You don't even have to think or question whether you need to trust or mistrust. They gave their word and that's it. If they said this is a monogamous relationship, you never have to think whether or not you need to trust them. Remember, you killed trust in the backyard with Andrea's gun!"

The ladies' eyes moved across the room falling on Andrea as they laughed. Andrea and I joined them as well.

"Trust is dead along with mistrust. You don't even have to trust whether or not your significant other's word is good. The two of you sit down and establish that it is your word that will make the relationship work. Once you say it, it is done. Imagine if you never have to doubt or think twice about what they say. And, they have the same with you. That is a very different mindset. It is an example of how integrity has power. In that kind of relationship, mistrust has no chance of survival. Neither is there any chance of another person dividing the two of you. Trust and mistrust are never considerations. All that matters is your word. Besides, your word is what makes any kind of relationship work."

"Okay," Andrea said. "That really is a different mindset."

Susan slid her hand across her forehead pretending to wipe away invisible sweat from her brow. "Whew," she said. "It's no nonsense, too. Ted, do you always make your relationships so complex? It's rhetorical; you don't have to answer; I already know."

"That's deep, Ted," was the final thought from Tasha.

Leslie posed another question, "Is that the kind of relationship you had with the woman you were just talking about?"

"I would say so. I was nineteen when she and I were in a relationship," I said. "My perspective about relationships was not as rich as it is now, even though I had a pretty good grip on relationships at that age."

Kelly quickly spoke up, asking another question. "From what you described, it took two people to make it such a great relationship. How old was she?"

"Twenty-one," I replied.

"Did she have the same ideals or values about relationships as you?" Andrea asked.

"That's a great question. I could not say for sure."

"Then how do you think the two of you were able to create the dynamic you had?" Susan interjected. "Most nineteen-year-olds are not thinking about having a great relationship. Somehow you were. What was behind that relationship? Better yet, how did you meet? Was it through a mutual friend or family? Maybe that had something to do with it. And what's her name?"

"She sounds lovely!" Tasha said.

"Do tell, Ted!" Kelly added.

"Her name was Lynette. No mutual friends or family. I met her in college. I went to Howard University, and I saw her at the first football game of the season. When the game was over, I walked up to her. When I looked at her, I thought I had seen her before. Except, I didn't want to use that line."

A few chuckles warmed the room, as my meeting with Lynette unfolded.

"It just so happened she and I were from the same state, New Jersey. Then I really thought I had seen her before. Nevertheless, I asked to walk her home. She said no because she had a jealous boyfriend. So, that was that."

"C'mon Ted! I know that can't be all you're going to tell us!" Susan's facetious anger provoked her to ask more questions. "That's all you're going to tell us?" she asked. "How did that turn into a relationship? Tell us more and don't leave out the juicy details! Right ladies! We want more! Ha ha!!"

Susan had incited the women to chant, as each one rippled agreement and chanted, "We want more!"

"Aren't you ladies nosy?" I held up my hands as I laughed, succumbing to their chant. "Okay. I'll tell you more."

With that, I continued my story. "I saw her several times on campus. I would go and talk to her for a few minutes. She was never available for more than a nice chat. When I went home for Christmas break, I saw her in a nightclub I frequented. She was with her boyfriend. In October of the next year, I saw her on campus. This time she appeared available. We exchanged numbers and went on a first date.

"While it was October in Washington DC, the weather can still be a bit warm, not hot. For the first time in my life, I was nervous on a date. I couldn't believe it. I was so nervous I was sweating like a pig wearing a winter coat in July. I was driving, and the entire back of my shirt was completely soaked, as though I ran five miles. The shirt was sky blue and kind of a silk material. So, one drop of water showed up quickly. She asked why I was sweating. I said, as I tried to play it cool, 'maybe I'm nervous'. She gave a nervous laugh and said, 'How do you know I'm not nervous, too.' We had a great first date that turned into a second a week later.

"For me, aside from the fact I felt as though I had known her my entire life, I was so turned on by her. While her physical appearance was extraordinary, there was more to it. She was so completely vulnerable with me, as though she had known me her entire life. To this day, I have never experienced a woman who allowed herself to be that vulnerable with me. I felt as though she literally laid her life in my hands. In a way, you could say that takes an enormous amount of trust. However, I had done nothing to earn her trust. It was that way from the beginning. At the same time, I felt as though she fully embraced and accepted the man I was.

"Now that we were in a relationship, I told her that I felt as though I had met her before. She said she felt as though she had met me as well. I asked if she ever went to Orange Park. She said she never went to that park. We went down a list of other places in New Jersey and never came up with a place that could have been common ground for us.

"At some point, Lynette returned to New Jersey. Years later, she said part of the reason she returned to New Jersey was to see if I would follow. She thought that would be a great way for me to demonstrate my seriousness for her. I did not want to go back yet. Maybe I could have stopped her from returning. I didn't because I always knew I could get her back. She was mine, even though I know you can't possess a person. There were other things I wanted to accomplish in my life. One of them was living abroad for many years.

"Over the years, I would see her in New Jersey or New York City—beach, nightclubs, parks, etc. And I was still obsessed with wanting to know where I first met her. Finally, the last time I spoke to her, I asked if she had ever gone to Rahway Park in New Jersey. She said 'yes.' Her father would drop her and her sister off at the swimming pool every summer and leave them there for the entire day. Every summer, I would go there with my family, including cousins, aunts and uncles, and have a cookout and swim in this huge swimming pool. I asked if she knew George. She said 'yes.' I went on to tell her the story of how George and I became friends.

"When I was eight, George walked up to me and said, 'Hi my name is George. Would you like to be my friend?' I hesitated at first because I was with my brother and cousins. And we had a tight bond, like cousin brothers. Yet, George's invitation for friendship was so innocent and inviting I said 'yes.' I introduced him to my brother and cousins. In the subsequent years, I introduced him to the adults in my family and invited him to eat with us.

"Without fail, George was at Rahway Park swimming pool every year. One year George asked me if I wanted to play with his friends. I said 'sure.' He introduced me to two girls who were our age. George and I played with them for a long time. The two girls were Lynette and her sister Jamie. Lynette's eyes never changed. I recognized them ten years later.

"I asked Lynette if she remembered that day. She said vaguely because George knew everyone. He was always introducing her and her sister to new friends."

"Wow! What a story," Susan said. "I didn't expect all that. Touching," she said, "very touching."

"It says a lot about you," Leslie added.

"Thank you," I said.

"That's deep and quite a story! Also says a lot about the times we live in. You can't leave your children anywhere all day," Tasha said.

"So true. I sometimes wonder if the times we live in are the major reason people have such a difficult time developing love relationships. It seems the more divorces and failed relationships that happen in society the more people are afraid of a failed relationship. That can have people, including children, starting relationships with the belief things just don't work out. Then there is the belief that relationships are hard work," I added more to the conversation.

Kelly sat up in her chair.

"Well," she said, "relationships do take work."

"And one-time people believed the earth was the center of the universe, and all the planets revolved around earth, and the earth was flat. As we now know, none of that was true," I said.

Kelly crossed her arms.

"What? What does that have to do with anything?" she asked.

"There are so many things that people believe, even though they are not true," I said, answering her question. I went on to say more, "So, I have a difficult time buying into that narrative of relationships being hard work. Nevertheless, you raise an important point. Regardless of what I think, if most believe it's hard, it will be. This is a good time to address this outdated philosophy. Before I go on about the great things I like when building a relationship, let's talk about why they fail. Then you will understand part of what makes relationships hard."

"Okay. That's been my experience," Kelly's arm rested on the chair. "Or at least I was always told relationships take hard work," she explained.

Why Relationships Fail

"I would like to discuss relationships in the context that all relationships are the result of learned behavior," I said.

"Sounds good! Let's hear it, Ted," Tasha's infectious smile spread across her face. The other ladies took a moment to freshen their drinks, go to the powder room, and answer texts. Tasha joined them.

Leslie yawned, stretching her neck from side to side, "I didn't realize how late it is," she said.

Andrea returned from the powder room, "I kinda feel like I'm at a seminar," she smiled as she sat. "I definitely want to hear more!"

The women returned and I resumed.

"The behavior is part of the human paradigm. Regardless of the country you live in or the language you speak there are common tenets that are shared by everyone. Also, in this context, relationships are not limited to love and intimacy. We are taught to believe that a relationship is made up of two personalities coming together. We even think certain personalities are more compatible with others. I say that is a myth, and I would like to dispel that myth and offer a new perspective on relationships."

"A myth?" Andrea questioned. "How is such a common belief a myth?" Andrea shifted in her seat and crossed her legs.

"When you and I wake up in the morning," I said, "your mind is listening to something that I will call a radio station. Almost everyone has a conversation going on in their head when they wake up. Some say it's too early. Others say it's Monday. There are many other conversations people wake up into. In fact, most of your attitudes and outlooks depend on those conversations in your head and are shaped by them. Except, where do those conversations come from? You and I did not invent them. By a certain age, each of you were given a radio station in your mind that you cannot turn off.

"Depending on your socioeconomic class, gender, race, age, country… you were born into a radio station that has certain dominant conversations. You think you are creating those conversations yourself. However, you had nothing to do with them. You were born into them. And worst of all, you do not even hear the radio station. You think it is you making up the conversation. Perhaps the reality is that the radio station conversations own you.

"Therefore, when two people meet, they believe they are connecting. Because they have been given the same or similar conversations to live into as reality, they believe they have chemistry. Conversely, those who are listening to a very different radio station may feel the other person does not understand them. It would be what people call a lack of chemistry," I explained.

"I think I get what you're saying now," Andrea said and leaned back with her glass in hand. "Please continue. I didn't mean to interrupt."

I sat there for a second composing the rest of my thoughts. The women waited in silence.

"Imagine two people coming together for love and their minds are listening to two very different radio stations that they cannot turn off. What they will be left with is 'my conversation in my head has the right solutions to life and your conversation is wrong.' There would be no possibility of creating power between the two of them. Real power requires people to invent from nothing. If two people wanted to build an extraordinary relationship, they would have to invent it without the predetermined facts about life and relationships. They would have to distinguish the station they were born into and choose between the conversations that have made them who they are and the person they would like to be. That may require letting go of the past. Except, letting go of the past is extremely difficult for most people. How many people say, 'This is who I am and there is nothing I can do about it?' Or 'I am nothing without my (you fill in the blank).' For most, letting go of the identity you were given is like dying. With no identity, people feel like they are nothing.

"Yet, people are willing to give up happiness, success, and love to hold on to a radio station that plays in their mind even though they had nothing to do with it. Unfortunately, many of those radio stations inform us to make poor decisions. Distinguish your station. Listen to the language you have in your mind—the type of words you use when problems show up. If you cannot hear your language, listen to the language of the people who are closest to you. They may be listening to the station that is on the same frequency as yours. If you want to be free, let it go!

"As you can see, everyone is listening to a radio station. There are certain things that are common to all humans. The human experience is very much the same for all healthy people. You are born, you have parents, you learn to walk, talk, feed yourself, read, write, arithmetic, etc. Furthermore, you eat, sleep, go to the bathroom, get happy, sad, angry, etc. I lived in several countries and could not find any people who lived outside of this paradigm, even when I lived in the jungle of Belize with Mayan Indians. There we had no electricity or running water. On the other end, I've dined with billionaires and had breakfast and lunch in the executive dining room of the New York Stock Exchange with the Chairman of the Board.

"No matter where I lived, people were adhering to the human paradigm. They believed certain things were impossible, like walking on air. And they believed killing was wrong. Some of the rules are so common that no one questions them. We are taught there is good and bad, up and down, dark and light, right and wrong, beautiful and ugly, push and pull, as well as many other concepts. That way of thinking focuses on duality and shapes everything we think, say, and do. However, we don't realize the extent to which it shapes who we are.

"Some of the ways you know you are listening to the radio station of duality is you have a conversation with yourself or another that focuses on the following things: **being right**—people would rather be right about their point of view instead of listening or negotiating with another; **making wrong**—to be right, the other must be wrong. Except, the other can only be wrong from your point of view; **defend**—you defend your position even when it is inappropriate; **prove**—If people do not prove themselves to you, you may not trust them. Or you may invalidate them; **validate**—you conjure up many philosophies to validate your existence at work, home or play; **invalidate**—You discredit another to validate yourself. Sometimes disagreement is designed to invalidate another; **justify**—even when your actions are inappropriate, you will make excuses to hide your actions. Or explain why someone is wrong to prove they deserved it; **dominate**—many people are obsessed with control; control is one way to dominate another; it can be done physically, financially, or verbally; **avoid domination**—there are times people avoid domination by attempting to dominate; other times they will abandon situations to avoid being dominated; in other cases, they will self sabotage a situation, including a successful career or love relationship."

"You're always saying deep stuff," Tasha said. "Do you always try to make people think so much?"

"I never know what people will think about what I say." Then while shrugging I added, "I'm only sharing."

"Okay. I'm cool with it. I like what you have to say. It's interesting. So, finish. Sorry for interrupting again. Please continue," Tasha said and sat back in her chair to wait for my response.

"Ha ha!" I chuckled without offense. "It's cool. I don't mind your input or questions," I said appreciating her openness." If you listen to yourself and others closely, you will begin to hear a pattern in the language of the radio station emerge. The words above eventually become part of the conversation, especially when there is a dispute or when things are not going the way you expected. Likely, one or all parties involved are listening to thoughts or conversations in their own mind about how they can be right, dominate, justify, etc. The goal of that language is to look good or avoid looking bad. Furthermore, if you can prove you are a victim, for example, you get to avoid any responsibility for any inappropriate behavior on your part. There are times when being a victim allows you to avoid domination. Other times it allows you to dominate.

"For me, one of the strangest phenomena is the conversation that occurs in the radio station of women. You are told that a man will dominate your life when you are in a relationship with him. He will want to confine you to the bedroom and kitchen. If you marry him, you give up your last name to take his. He will physically and financially dominate you. He will dominate your thoughts and change you. As a result, many women have devised plans to avoid being dominated by men.

"Once a woman believes she must protect herself from a perceived threat of being dominated by a man, she will defend herself. If something happens that might appear to be the least bit domineering, she will be able to justify inappropriate actions to avoid being dominated. This mindset puts a relationship in conflict before it starts. What's amazing is if two women are best friends, they will influence one another's thoughts and behaviors. That is not considered domination. If a man, however, attempts to influence his significant other's thoughts or behaviors, he is a domineering man," I said.

"My turn to interrupt," Kelly said raising her hand. "That's an interesting comparison of domination."

"If I hear Ted correctly, perhaps domination may be a strong word for us to digest. Influence, I think is better," Leslie added.

"Yeah, I like the term influence better, "Tasha agreed, "not as harsh."

"I can see how you girls would see it like that. Domination has an assigned meaning that is interpreted as derogatory," Susan explained further. "Please continue, Ted."

Responding, I said, "I ask that you consider, the radio station is speaking for all of you. It just went into defense mode. Your responses are examples of how automatic the radio station is. In fact, your radio stations are dominating each of you. I will get to that later. To continue what I was a saying, from another perspective, if your significant other is incapable of influencing your life, why are you with them? What better person to contribute to your life than your significant other?" I asked, then continued. "These are just some of the hidden aspects of life that can derail relationships. They are like minefields. In fact, these elements of the radio station can blow up any relationship—business, family, or love. While you can be aware there are minefields, if you are unable to distinguish them, there is nothing you can do about them. Here I have given you some tools to distinguish them. These tools give you the power to do something about the minefields built into the radio station that every healthy person inherits.

"For those who believe they did not inherit those elements, the fact you believe they are not part of your life is an example of how the radio station runs the show. It runs your life and remains hidden from you. In fact, the radio station becomes such a part of you that you believe it is you. Instead of realizing you have tendencies to be right or make others wrong and dominate or avoid being dominated, you—or better said—the radio station, will prove and defend itself. Furthermore, the denial to distinguish the radio station in your mind is a way to avoid being dominated by it. If you attempt to run from it, that would simply be a way to avoid being dominated by it.

"That also says something about your ability to distinguish the elements that influence your life. Once you distinguish the radio station, you will realize that the station is not your voice. It will be the voices of friends, family, and media.

The elements of the radio station serve a purpose. They allow you to look good or avoid looking bad. In your career, you are trained and expected to conduct yourself according to the rules of professionalism in the workplace. When you follow those rules, you look good. When it comes to your personal life, there is no training. You do whatever is necessary to avoid looking like a fool. That includes manipulation. Too often, people will damage their love relationship to look good to their friends and family. Yet, some of that behavior would be out of bounds in the business world. While that same behavior will get you fired at work, you believe it is acceptable with your significant other," I finished my thought.

"You got that right!" Susan said. "It's unbelievable how stupid some people act in a relationship. It's not children that need to be sent to the time out room. It's that guy or girl."

Susan clapped her hands in laughter. The other women joined her.

Between laughs, Andrea managed to say, "I hear what you're saying, Ted. But sometimes men do try to control you. Like Susan said, that's when you want to send them to the time out room, even when you love them." she began to laugh again.

I laughed, too. "The key is to know when you are doing it, even you," I pointed at Andrea, teasing her. Observation told me that she wouldn't remain silent. She didn't disappoint me.

"Me?" pointing at herself, she feigned surprise and innocence. "I would never try to control a man." She laughed cocking her head to the side. "I don't have to. Us women have a secret weapon that all straight men respond to."

Another fit of laughter hit her and the ladies. "Ha ha!" she said." Just joking! Just joking! That was the radio station talking, not me. Ha ha!" she added.

"You're crazy, Andrea!" Kelly teased, shaking her head.

"Can you use that secret weapon at work?" I asserted.

Andrea raised her eyebrows. "Some women do. I wouldn't suggest it. It can backfire," she said.

"You think so?" I asked.

"It sure can," Susan said with conviction. "She doesn't get what she expected. She used her body like she was making a transaction. When it backfires—that is, like you said, Ted, when the radio station screams 'I'm a victim'—that woman does not have to take responsibility for misusing her body for career or financial gain."

"Some may even call her unprofessional," was my response.

The women in the room all offered an affirmation. Nodding their heads, sipping from their glasses, saying," True."

"So, most people at work learn to exhibit professional behavior. Even though people manipulate one another at work. They lie, cheat, and steal. There is a certain protocol at work that is the standard," I said.

"I've always been amazed that people will treat coworkers or even strangers better than their spouse. People justify it by saying they are only human. What if you could be a professional husband/wife or boyfriend/girlfriend? Many may find that idea stale, confining, distasteful or unappealing. At the same time, people know that the inappropriate language or behavior they display in their love lives would alienate them at work. That includes temper tantrums, yelling, demeaning remarks, or physical abuse. While I understand there are isolated incidents in the workplace where people become violent—physically or verbally, those people are eventually fired. If not, that organization may develop a reputation for being a dangerous place to work. And therefore, may not attract or retain top talent. However, many intimate relationships are filled with behaviors that are deemed inappropriate in the workplace. And still those perpetrators of bad behavior can find a mate who will tolerate it.

"If, on the other hand, everyone was to conduct themselves in a relationship with the same professionalism they have with a client, I am willing to bet the divorce rate would drop instantly. Why? First, people practice greater scrutiny when hiring a new employee. You are trained to look for someone with a specific kind of experience. You also look for work ethic and values that support the culture of the enterprise. That requires getting to know the person with questions. You want to make sure the prospective hire understands the demands of the position. And you want to be assured they are a good fit and can fulfill the company's mission," I concluded.

"Ted, you got me thinking about something. You talk about being a professional spouse. Now that's interesting. But, I wonder if most people even know what their spouse does in their profession. Do you think most men or women could give you details about their significant other's occupation? I don't mean they have to be an expert," Susan asked.

"Those are great questions," I said. "I would add something to that. Can you advocate for your mate?" I asked. Not waiting for an answer, I went on to say, "There is a book and movie called, *Barbarians at the Gate*. It's about the actual 1988 leverage buyout of RJR Nabisco by the investment management firm Kohlberg, Kravis Roberts (KKR). Henry Kravis is Co-CEO of KKR, and F. Ross Johnson was the CEO of RJR Nabisco. In the movie, Johnson meets with the CEO of American Express, Jim Robinson, to secure financing through their Shearson Lehman division to buy his own company from public shareholders. It later became the largest leverage buyout in history at that time. In the end, Kravis of KKR bought the company. It was about a $26 billion deal.

"In the scene where F. Ross Johnson and his wife met for lunch with the American Express CEO, Jim Robinson and his wife, Linda. During lunch, Linda asked if her public relations company could handle RJR Nabisco's PR for the leverage buyout that Johnson was about to initiate. Throughout the movie, Linda was aware of every step that took place in the deal. While in the end, Johnson lost his job and company and the Robinson's lost the deal and Kravis of KKR won, Jim and Linda Robinson were a shining example of a married couple being a powerful team in their professional lives. In the movie, it appeared both Linda and Jim were extremely aware of what each other did in their careers. And they could advocate for one another. It appears, as a team, they added value to one another, as well as to their respective clients.

"The movie is an excellent example of what happens when couples acknowledge one another as professionals. It doesn't mean you have to be an expert at your significant other's profession. It's simply important to know enough so you can advocate for them. And I don't mean in the sense of being a cheerleader. In the movie, the CEO of American Express had enough confidence in his wife to bring her along to important business meetings revolving around the leverage buyout. In fact, she was part of several confidential meetings throughout the movie. It is highly unlikely she would have been part of those meetings if she were not the wife of the American Express CEO." This time I paused to watch the reactions of the ladies. Everyone seemed engrossed, so I kept talking.

"While it's a great point you brought up, Susan, I don't want to lose my train of thought. I was talking about the differences between people being a professional at work from being unprofessional in an intimate relationship. I was saying people practice greater scrutiny when they interview prospective employees. Second, there is no game about why the person is being interviewed. You don't entertain a person because you have nothing else to do. During that interview, if there is mutual interest, it is expressed.

"Third, there are background checks. The hiring company wants to understand what kind of person they are about to hire. That can be confirmation for integrity, experience, or education. While none of these steps guarantees a great hire, there is a committed effort to understand whom you are bringing into the lives of people in the company. The fact background checks are done is an impetus for people to be on their best behavior at work. No one wants to develop a bad reputation. It could impede career growth or hurt chances of getting hired in another company. Once again, looking good and avoid looking bad," I said.

"So, what's wrong with that?" Tasha asked. "You have to pay the bills and eat. So, you do what is right at work."

"I'm not making it right or wrong," I said. "I'm asking you to look at behavior. For some reason, when it comes to intimate relationships, people put too much emphasis on external factors, like physical attractiveness and financial security. Because people are enamored with external factors, they are less diligent about making sure there is a match. The result is a compromise. They believe things magically happen because chemistry is the mystical elixir that changes everything. Or they believe they can change the person themselves. When it doesn't work, they express their disappointment, when in fact it was the interviewing process that was flawed," I said.

"Okay. Point noted. I'll do background checks on the next man I date," Tasha said.

I continued, "In addition, even if the correct person is brought into your intimate life, there are fewer boundaries than at work."

Like a ripple effect everyone posed the question, "Like what?"

"For example, if things are not going the way you like in the office, it is not acceptable to yell at people or withhold your work. Whatever your contribution is, it can affect everyone in the company if you decide you want to sit and pout for eight hours. Your work is a product, whether it's finance, sales, human resources, assembly line, etc. In a relationship, your product is love, affection, and acknowledgement. If you decide you are no longer producing what the relationship needs to prosper, you have quit or are on strike. Quitting means you are leaving. On strike requires talks to negotiate terms that work for everyone," I said.

"You love negotiating," Tasha said.

"Yet, people remain in relationships without producing love, affection, or acknowledgement. They play tit for tat; you didn't give me what I want, so I won't give you what you want. In other cases, they communicate by yelling or manipulating," I said.

"Okay. I see what you mean. It would be better to talk than to do what you said—quit or go on strike," Tasha said.

"If, however," I continued, "you were trained to be a professional husband, for example, you would know how to conduct yourself with a level of professionalism that will get you a raise and/or promotion from your wife. You would serve her as though she were your client. As a client, she has the right to make demands if she continues to pay for the services. In business, those terms are negotiated. When a client demands change, so will the terms of payment. If a husband approached his wife with the mindset of professionalism, he would always be concerned about her needs. He would make client calls to ensure her needs are being met. And he would schedule meetings or lunches that are designed for him to anticipate changing needs. More importantly, she would be his biggest and most important client,"

"I think all women would love that," Kelly added

"The wife, on the other hand, would want to keep this vendor. The vendor or husband solves problems for her. Three of his deliverables are love, affection, and acknowledgement. This relationship works when it's vice versa. The husband is the client of the wife. In the event things are not going as anticipated, professional behavior does not allow for immediate dismissal. It requires conversations. Those conversations require a tremendous amount of listening on both parts. Furthermore, instead of annual reviews, you provide real time feedback when things are working well or not working to your satisfaction.

"An example from my professional life goes as follows. I ran a transportation logistics company. I acquired a new client that had a major presence in the global marketplace. When I met with the decision maker, she said they used six companies like mine in the past three months. In a dismissive way, she told me if I wanted to be number seven be my guest. For ten months, we were flawless. Then we made a mistake that cost that client money. The decision maker reluctantly had to fire us. I called her and asked how many of our competitors could service you for ten months without a single hiccup? She said 'none.' I told her I would make sure flawless services continued. To do that, she and I agreed on new ways to service her company. Some of those new ways required us to charge more. Until I left the company, we continued to provide extraordinary service to that client. And her initial dismissive behavior changed to very pleasant and welcoming.

"By conducting myself as a professional, the money continued to flow from the client. With that said, why would I treat my significant other with less respect than I treat a client. Is money more important than love, affection, and acknowledgement? When I treat my significant other with the same level of respect I give to a client, love, affection, and acknowledgement flows daily. When my significant other provides the same to me, I am more effective at dealing with clients, friends, and family. When my relationship with my significant other is acrimonious, I am less effective in other aspects of my life. That would make my significant other the most important person in my life, even though I value my professional life.

"Becoming a professional in your intimate relationship has enormous advantages. However, choosing the right person to share all aspects of your life must be as important, if not more, as hiring someone in a business. After all, the love of your life is responsible for bringing value to your life in the same way a new hire does for their job," I said.

"Wow!" Susan jumped up, glass in hand. She walked over to refill her drink, finishing what she was saying. "You gave us an entire case study. You better write a book about this conversation. You always come up with these great and unique perspectives for relationships. With all that said, being a professional may be easier said than done," she said. "Anybody want a refill while I'm up?"

Ice clinked in her glass, as she prepared her beverage. The ladies offered a chorus of 'no thank you,' as Andrea joined her to mix her drink. "Ted?"

"No, thank you. I'm okay for now." I went on to elaborate on the conversation. "Maybe." Was my response to the idea of writing a book. "Remember I asked if you would hire an inexperienced and noncredentialled person as a CPA," I asked. "A qualified CPA would be trained. We have no training to make one a professional husband or wife. Everyone is poking around in the dark. No pun intended. Maybe that's why some people say love hurts."

"Ha ha! I caught that pun," Susan threw her head back and laughed a heartier laugh. " I was going to say something."

The other ladies laughed as well.

"So who decides what a professional is? In other words, who sets the standard for professional husband or wife behaviors?" Susan asked. "Imagine that question about being an engineer or psychologist. It seems the market has decided. In the world we live in, it would most likely be the best marketers of the training. Isn't that how people choose a significant other? Women choose the guy who markets himself the best. He may be lousy at relationships. However, he knows how to say exactly what she wants to hear. He reads the script that makes her comfortable. When you think about it, it's funny. Watching men and women come together is like watching a Broadway play. Everyone knows their lines," I said.

"Well it's not funny when a woman later finds out the only thing the guy has to offer is a few good lines," Andrea said.

"That even happens in the workplace. Some people interview well. When you hire them, they are mediocre at best. In other cases, they completely lied about their experience. Companies have policies to handle that. They train them up, put them in another area or fire them," I said.

Kelly was quiet, distracted by her phone, while Tasha sent a text, yawning, as she resettled into her chair. The fire flickered lightly, catching Susan's attention. She quietly got up to tend to it, turning the propane up to reignite the fire over the rocks.

"It's not so easy to just fire a man from your life. A woman has feelings involved," Leslie added.

"I can see that," I said. "As I mentioned, women's brains secrete more oxytocin than men's. Therefore, she bonds faster. At the same time, you get one life. Who do you want to spend it with?" I asked the room.

Leslie, waving her hand, said, "See, this is the part of you that makes you sound cold. On average, people are not that cut and dry."

"That's why I suggest you have thorough conversations up front. If a person misrepresents, they must know there are consequences," I insisted.

Leslie sighed, "The mindset you have could make a woman believe she has to be perfect."

"How?" I asked.

"There isn't much room for error with you. She has to be on point all the time. Otherwise, you could say she misrepresented herself and now you have grounds to terminate the relationship," Leslie said.

"People get fired from jobs every day. That doesn't stop them from seeking employment," I said.

"There's that 'so what' attitude," Susan said.

"Not really," I said. "Life has risks. If you really want to avoid all risks, stay home alone and never leave the house. When a woman has poor criterion for a man, it may be because she is not sure of what she wants in a man or a relationship. Because she does not know, she is an easy target for a player. The player is someone who's 'got game.' Women have been indoctrinated with the idea that men must have 'game' to get her. In the woman's mind, having can be a sign that the man is making effort. Women believe they are worth a man's effort. What most women don't realize is that men who have 'game' have it because they have to."

"What?" Tasha asked. "Why do they have to?"

"They have nothing else to offer. They spend too much of their time figuring out how to chase a woman. They haven't dedicated the same time for how to build and maintain a great relationship," I explained.

"Many women learn that the hard way. A lot never learn. They make themselves available for one guy after another. Each man having 'game,'" I finished my explanation.

"That's another way to look at a guy with 'game.' Some might say what you just said is smooth 'game,'" Tasha laughed.

"Maybe. I would rather develop myself to give and receive what I want. Besides, it takes two to make a relationship work. Therefore, the effort to get to know one another is the responsibility of both. If I, as a man, am the only one responsible for making the effort, what I am learning about you and what you offer as a partner is nothing. From another perspective, women set up the game to be disappointed. The game of 'chase me' is like cat and mouse. It seems many women do not understand the rules of cat and mouse. The cat chases the mouse. When it catches the mouse, it plays with it. At some point, it will hurt the mouse, and the mouse will not move very well. As soon as the cat sees another healthy mouse, it will drop the hurt mouse for the new one that presents a chase. That cycle never ends. The man's brain has been programmed to find joy in the chase. That could result in a series of unstable relationships where he damages the relationship to the point the woman leaves. Then he must chase her again. Or he will be the eternal player who chases women for the rest of his life," I said.

"You give a lot to think about. Some guys are just good at hiding who they really are," Andrea said as she uncrossed her legs and sipped slowly from her glass.

"That's an excuse for two things. One, a woman does not know what she wants. Two, she did not ask real questions to ensure this guy could deliver what she wants. The funny thing is women are overly concerned about a man only wanting sex. That puts a woman in a defensive mode. It's hard to get to know someone who is in defense mode. The guy has to devise strategies to overcome artificial barriers. In other words, it is often women who make the relationship about sex. Instead of getting to know the guy, she is engaged in a chess match. They each make moves. He believes his goal is to get her in bed. Her goal is to make him work for the opportunity to sleep with her. During that time, they are not authentically getting to know one another. Sex has become the focal point, end game and distraction.

"Perhaps it would be better if they both said 'I like you and I'm sexually attracted to you. At the same time, I'm not ready for that right now. I enjoy sex and I would want to have great sex with you. At this point, I don't feel we have a strong enough bond for great sex. So, let's spend time focusing on creating that bond. That will require us to get to know one another well. Can we do that?' That approach takes the focus off sex and onto the individuals," I said.

Susan shook her head yes and said, "I could live with that approach. It sounds honest and mature. So, I agree. We do put too much emphasis on sex. I think actual sex and the idea of sex can blind us, especially women. For guys, they start thinking with the wrong head."

"Maybe it's time to stop saying guys think with the wrong head," I said. "As a rule, men and women do not have mature conversations around sex. For me, it's mind boggling that we don't. We act as though sex is some taboo that can't be discussed in the beginning. What makes that ridiculous is that the overwhelming majority of us on the planet are here because two people engaged in sexual intercourse. Without sex we wouldn't be here. So, what's the big deal?" I paused. "Besides," I continued, "how many women would stay in a love relationship with a man who refused to have sex with her? If men and women were mature about sex, they would discuss it up front. They would say something like I mentioned above to acknowledge there is sexual interest. It would simply be better if we spend time getting to know one another first.

"Instead, sex becomes a game and secretly the focal point. The guy pursues sex. The woman avoids it. All the while both are pretending that it is not happening. What's worse is the woman decides when it will or will not happen. How can sex be mutual if only one party decides when it will happen? That's analogous to going to the store with your parents, and they decide whether you get candy. Adulthood allows you to go to the store and buy candy when you want. At the least, it would be much more mature if a man could ask a woman what she needs to be comfortable to become sexually active with him. In that conversation, they both get to decide how soon sex can happen. The way it's set up now a woman would claim she is being pressured to have sex. And the man must back off if he wants to keep her interest. If he persists, he is accused of thinking with his other head. The current relationship platform is too small and one sided."

"I can see why a man would say that. That would be a more mature approach. To do that, you need mature people. Not everyone is mature enough to handle that kind of honest conversation. Also, women are taught to be less interested in sex. When a woman expresses strong desires for sex, there is a negative stereotype for her," Kelly said.

"The social dynamics between men and women were set up exactly as they are. We are taught to suppress. And we accept this as reality. At some point, it would be wise for us to realize Puritans set up this country called the USA. They were very suppressive. England kicked them out because they were so suppressive. Yet, we still have the cultural values they imposed on the land mass now called the United States. And no one questions this so-called reality. That's no different than the times when astronomers said the earth was the center of the universe and all the planets revolved around it. They accepted that as reality without questioning it. We are not stuck with the way things are," I said.

"Now that we're on sex, there is something to add to that. One of my concerns, and I know it's not a fact, is if a woman is not making an effort in the beginning of getting to know me, she may not know how to make the effort when it comes to love making. This idea of being the prize because you're a woman is unfulfilling for a man. I want to be engaged by her, intellectually and sexually. If she is waiting for me to 'do it' to her, I'm not really getting as much out of sex as she may think. Sex is not really about the climax. And the climax does not mean a man is sexually satisfied. It goes back to the building blocks of this conversation: love, affection, and acknowledgement.

"I want to be acknowledged sexually. You can't acknowledge me if you are being an observer to see 'what I got' in bed. In other words, you can't just lie there. Great sex is no different than the entire relationship. It takes two. That means a woman has to know her body well. Unfortunately, most men and women believe that they have something special to offer when it comes to sex. When it comes to sex, it's no different than a love relationship. Without training, you may not be that good at it. And having a lot of sex partners does not automatically make you good. It could have the reverse effect, especially if you were with people who also were not good. So first, as a woman, learn your body," I said.

"That's true. A lot of women don't know their bodies," Susan added.

"Second, learn mine. Third, affection and intimacy are extremely important," I said.

"When it comes to love, well, love is not always a mandatory element of great sex. It helps though, especially if both are fully engaged and know their bodies. From another perspective, if a woman markets herself as a sex goddess with the best goods in town and she lied, I can treat her in the same way as a job candidate. I can fire her. I can retrain her. Or I can reposition her in my life, like make her a friend."

"I was with you until you said this reposition stuff," Kelly said.

"That would make me a professional boyfriend seeking a professional girlfriend. She just lied on her resumé. And she interviewed well by stretching the truth. There are consequences for that," I said.

"I guess. No woman would want to be treated that way," Susan offered her reply.

"What way?" I asked.

"Well, told that she is fired, repositioned, or retrained," Susan replied.

"Thank you, Susan! You said exactly what I was thinking," Tasha added.

"I agree with them, Ted. No one wants to hear that," Leslie said.

Andrea and Kelly nodded in agreement.

"People are fired from relationships all the time. It's called divorce," I defended my statement. "What's wrong with retraining?" I added. "Maybe she does not know her body as well as she thinks. Believe it or not, I see that a lot. In fact, some women have told me that because I was not a woman, there is no way I could understand what she is feeling during sex. However, there are certain bodily functions and sensations that happen in all healthy women. Just because you don't know about it, does not mean it can't happen. In that situation, the woman had to learn things about her body that she didn't even know she didn't know. Once it's explored, that can be a great journey for both of us. It becomes unfortunate when she is unwilling to explore. When she is willing, it creates an even stronger bond between us. The idea of retraining also applies if the woman believes all men enjoy sex the same way. She will have to learn my body and what is pleasurable to me," I said.

"Ted, can I ask you something personal?" Tasha asked.

"Sure," I said.

"Did you have to retrain Lynette?" she asked.

"Wow! That *is* personal. The answer is no. I always felt she was completely uninhibited. She was so vulnerable with me that anything could happen. It was otherworldly with her in a very intimate way."

"Whew! That sounds deep. Why do you think it was that way?" Tasha said.

"I don't have a cut and dry answer. Maybe I don't have an answer that would satisfy anyone," I said. "I will say that she knew her body and how to enjoy it with me. She was also very interested in pleasing me. However, she did it without trying. She was just a very engaging lover."

"I can see that being a very deep and satisfying relationship," Andrea said.

"It was. I'd like to segue sex into something more powerful," I said.

"What would that be?" Andrea asked.

"I think we all agree that sex is very powerful," Tasha submitted.

"Earlier I said sex is not just for the climax. Sex is a big part of the body's normal functions. It is as normal as eating, sleeping, and going to the bathroom. When we abstain, it can create problems in our bodies. Because it is so important, it can also support positive effects for the brain and body. During sex, different parts of the brain are stimulated. They have found that people who participate in regular sexual activity tend to have their creativity enhanced. They also have healthier bodies. In fact, there are statistics that say couples that have sex four days a week or more earn higher incomes and have happier marriages," I said.

"Who wouldn't be happier with more sex, especially if it is good?" Susan posed the question. "Maybe you should have said more sex equals love, affection, and acknowledgement."

"More sex does work wonders," I laughed, agreeing with Susan. "With that said, when you have a happier marriage, healthier body, and more creative mind, you are best positioned to live a life of abundance. When sex is intentionally withheld, think of it as robbing the family bank account. Withholds set up a life of scarcity. The scarcity mindset is the pathway to struggles, frustration, and poverty. It is much easier to build a thriving company or move up the corporate ladder with the abundance mindset.

"As you can see, sex is an aspect of life that contributes to satisfaction in many facets of life. If you observe many of the successful people in business, they often have a supportive significant other on their arm. Whether it's Henry Ford, John D. Rockefeller, Sr., or Oprah, they have someone who empowers them in the privacy of their homes. Informally, it is rumored that many of the successful titans have huge sex drives. As I said in the beginning of this conversation, give your significant other what they want."

"I guess you had to get that one in. Pun intended. Was that a cheap plug for all the men in the world?" Andrea said.

"Have you forgotten Cleopatra?" I asked. "Her sex drive was out of this world."

"Okay. We get the picture. Sex is important. I also like something you said earlier. You talked about intimacy in sex and how important it is to understand that sex starts before the bedroom. That's an example of two people who are operating as one in and out of the bedroom," Kelly said.

"It is," I agreed.

"You also talked about how affection is not always about foreplay. That's important because, even as a woman, sometimes you are not in the mood for foreplay. You want to just get it on. If you know what I mean?" Kelly said.

"I do."

Kelly went on, "What I find to be an extremely important point that you made is that sex is an intricate part of our lives. It is so important that it not only affects our relationship with our significant other, but also affects how we interact with the rest of the world. As you said, having the scarcity or abundant mindset can make the difference between failure, mediocrity, or extraordinary success. So, I'm wondering about people who have had a successful marriage for forty to fifty years. I wonder what they would have to say about that. It would be interesting to hear their take on how their sexuality contributed to happy marriages and successful careers. I would love to get input from people like that."

"That would make for a great conversation. It would be great to get people who have been married that long in a room with people in their twenties and thirties," I replied.

"I think you're saying something else, Ted," Leslie said.

"What is that?" I asked.

"As a woman, it is freeing to know you are with a man who accepts you without judgment when it comes to sex. As I said, women can be different. It can be the same woman who becomes different with a different man or the same man." Leslie went on, "So, if she happens to have strong sexual desires with the man she loves, it would be empowering for her to not be judged as a nymphomaniac or some other derogatory word. It's that lack of judgment that can allow a woman to freely express herself. When she's judged, she may feel as though she is walking on eggshells. Then she may attempt to manipulate the man because she feels so constrained." She paused." Does that make sense, Ted?" she added.

"It does," I replied. "Then she doesn't want to look bad. That would be more instructions from the radio station."

"How? Are you blaming the woman?" Leslie asked.

"No. I'm blaming no one. Throughout this entire conversation, I've been talking about the need to have mature conversations," I said.

"True," Leslie remarked. "So, you're saying a woman should talk to the man about her sex drive? 'Hey honey, I like sex a lot. Are you comfortable with that?'"

"I know, right?! I totally agree with what Leslie is saying!" Tasha exclaimed.

"That's one way," I said, laughing with them. "Believe it or not," I continued, "there are guys who complain their wives want sex too much. Sometimes both men and women need to learn the art of seduction. Men like to be seduced as much as a woman does."

"I get your point. I like to be seduced. How should I seduce a man?" Leslie leaned forward, waiting for my answer.

"There is no one size fits all. Being feminine goes a long way." I raised my hand in protest. "Please don't ask me what it means to be feminine," I added.

"I wasn't," Leslie laughed at my false protest.

"You said something earlier in our conversation about offering a woman freedom to be herself. Or you said you offer a woman the freedom to be someone she hasn't been. I would say that could play a huge role in the amount of love making, as well as happiness, in the relationship/marriage," Tasha said.

"I can relate to that," I said.

"Would you also agree that sense of freedom is for both people? Now that could be Christmas every day," Tasha inquired.

"It surely would be," I replied. "And yes, sense of freedom is for both. I've always thought a relationship is best when it is the one place in the world where you can be yourself. Except, many people shy away from that when they think about being fully themselves. Most people believe being themselves includes bad behavior. Some of those people believe a significant other has to be strong to deal with them. That's just an excuse for plain old irresponsibility and immaturity. It's why I spent so much time talking about being a professional husband or wife. Being yourself includes constantly developing yourself and being responsible for the impact you have on your significant other. The same way you are expected to be an adult at work is the same way to be an adult in a relationship."

"Yes, since adulthood isn't what everyone brings to the table, it would be a great Christmas present for your mate, especially if you presented adulthood every day," Susan said.

"It surely would be a great present. However, people are so ready with the excuse 'I'm only human.' In some ways, that's playing victim to being human. That's a way of saying 'I'm helpless and can't do anything about it. The human paradigm is making me irresponsible and immature.' It's funny when you think about it."

"It's a little funny, but it's not funny when you experience someone's irresponsibility and immaturity. I would rather receive the Christmas present of being free with responsibility and maturity. Without it, relationships can seem like a bad idea and a loooooooot of work," Andrea stressed.

"Then let's start the relationship school. How to create an extraordinary relationship where every day is Christmas," I said.

Leslie raised her hand. "Sign me up!" she cried.

"Andrea, you brought up something important. I want to go back to something."

"What's that?" Andrea asked.

"You said relationships could seem like a bad idea and a lot of work. Kelly said the same earlier. I want to peel another layer on why relationships fail," I said.

"Okay. What layer is that? We could dedicate an entire book on why that happens. What do you have in mind?" Andrea questioned me.

"Infidelity," I responded.

"Well, that's an ugly topic. And it's one that surely needs to be addressed. I'm interested in hearing your thoughts on that as a man," Andrea admitted.

"We just started talking about adulthood and being responsible for your actions," I said.

"Okay. Sometimes it seems people make so many excuses for cheating you wonder if they are trying to convince themselves that they are doing the right thing. That's a way to avoid being responsible for anything," Susan remarked.

"It sure is. Now I want to be responsible for what I'm communicating to women with my words in this conversation between us. You ladies may believe I've been hard on all women with my straight talk. I'm only stating where I stand as a man. Now I want to address the fellas," I said.

"Oh, this will be interesting," Susan stated, sounding intrigued.

"It will be interesting! It's time for the men to get a dose of Ted's straight talk, for sure," Tasha added.

"Yes, I definitely want to hear your perspective regarding the men, too," Kelly said.

"Me, too," Leslie said.

"My hat is in the ring with the other ladies," Andrea managed to say along with the other women.

"I'll tell a true story first," I said.

"You have so many stories," Susan commented.

"I was once in a room with about fifteen guys. Out of nowhere, I said that men who cheat need to learn to ask their significant other to give them what they want. Every guy in the room looked at me as though I was a traitor. They responded as though I had broken some 'man code' of ethics. They mostly told me that I didn't understand. They told me I hadn't been in a relationship long enough. I told them I lived with a woman for five years. When they heard that, they all attempted to justify their actions. I continued to say that they needed to learn to ask for what they wanted when it comes to their spouse.

"Finally, one of the guys said, 'he (Ted) is right. We should have asked for what we wanted. But, when we got married, we were young and didn't know what we wanted. So we couldn't ask for it'. The other guys said 'that's true.' Except, they didn't say much more. I wasn't sure if some of them knew what they wanted at this point in their lives. Therefore, it is critical to understand yourself. That helps you understand what value you bring to another's life. And it helps you better assess what kind of person you want in your life, as well as what you want from them."

"That's an interesting story. It doesn't sound like you were too popular that day, Ted," Susan remarked.

"I wasn't," I said. "That was not my concern. I was coming from a certain state of mind."

"What's that?" Susan asked.

"Responsibility," I answered. "As a society," I continued, "we make so many excuses and then attribute it to only being human. We say it's only human to cheat. We even talk about how humans were not made to be with one person. It's never about cheating or being with one person. It's about your word. If you make an agreement with your significant other, keep your word."

"That's why trust is so important," Andrea commented.

"That's why I talked earlier about the importance of killing trust. If you depend on trust, mistrust is waiting around the corner to take over the relationship. People would be better off if they practiced keeping their word. If you kill trust, you only depend on your word."

"That's true. That is such an uncommon and counterintuitive way to think," Andrea said.

"It sure is. But it's really deep when you think about it," Tasha added. "Because we are taught that trust is so important, you need to constantly remind yourself to kill trust. I've never heard of killing trust before."

"I understand that," I said. "Just because one belief is imposed on us does not mean we have to stay with it forever. Remember, at one time, it was common sense to believe the earth was the center of the universe."

All five women nodded in agreement. "That's true," they intermittently affirmed.

"In other words, I'm concerned about people who cheat. If you will cheat on your spouse, what will stop you from cheating in other aspects of your life? Those fifteen guys in the room with me were raised in a society that says it's normal to cheat. And it's not only men who cheat. Many women do as well. And it's all justified, at least in their minds. People make analogies to animals. Or they blame their spouse for not doing things. Some guys cheat because they believe their wife dominates them. Cheating can be a way to avoid being dominated. The list of reasons goes on. If I'm honest with you, I've been the other guy. In other words, I've been the single guy sleeping with another man's wife or girlfriend. When I asked her why she was with me, she said that her husband might be cheating as well. She had no proof though.

"From another perspective, I once worked with a guy who was married. He had an agreement with his wife that every Friday he could go out alone to play. He could have sex with others. While I have no interest in judging that marriage, that man had the guts to sit down with his wife and tell her what he needed. And they had an agreement. If he stuck with one day a week, he wasn't cheating. That's a guy keeping his word. And that's a relationship with integrity, regardless of another's personal feelings about ethics and morals. It was their agreement."

"That is another way to be married," Kelly said. "Not for me though. I guess she could play if she wanted to," Kelly shrugged.

"I never inquired if that was the case. I'm only saying I respect a man who can have that kind of tough conversation with his wife."

"Yes," Susan was agreeable, "it's better to do that up front than to have to explain after getting caught. Getting caught can damage the relationship. As you say, it allows mistrust to come in and run the show," she said.

"It does. It could also kill or damage the partnership."

"It can. But what do you mean?" Andrea asked.

"I worked for a consulting firm. The president of the company was married to a woman who was a great partner for him," I explained. "They had a son. So, she was the soccer mom. At the soccer games, she would have conversations with the other moms. I assume she asked the usual questions. However, I think she was intentional about asking what their husbands did. His wife met a woman who was married to the CEO of a financial firm. The wife of the president—my employer—invited the husband and wife of the financial firm for dinner at their home. The wife of my company's president cooked a fantastic meal and the husbands had an opportunity to get to know one another well. Because of the dinner, the president of my company secured a consulting project with the financial firm. It later became his largest account. Technically speaking, his wife made that happen. The wife was the salesperson and they worked as a team to close the deal.

"That's another example of your mate being able to advocate for you. I don't think his wife made that happen by accident. I believe she had done the same in the past. So, she was very intentional when it came to supporting her husband's success. Even though she was a soccer mom, she was knowledgeable about her husband's business and knew how to help him grow it. In the end, she benefits. They eventually moved to a larger home."

"Wow!!! That's a great story and a great example of a couple working together," Leslie said.

"It's also an example of a couple building something together," I added.

"It sure is," Leslie remarked.

"It's kind of hard to do that if you're focused on infidelity," I said. "While I understand you can cheat on your spouse and still have a successful career, it will never beat having your spouse stand for you like the consulting firm or the CEO of American Express did for his wife."

The women nodded in agreement.

"There is a book called *The Millionaire Mind* by Thomas Stanley. In the book, he dedicated chapters to married millionaires. He said the divorce rate amongst millionaires was extremely low. He said most believe it's low because of the amount of money involved. After interviewing millionaire couples, he found their successful marriages had nothing to do with money. He said they were together because they shared many common values. It was the values that kept them together even when they did not have money. He gave several examples of couples that made money and lost everything and later made a fortune. His point was that even when they lost everything, they stayed together. That's an example of people having common values, taking a stand for one another and working as partners to build something."

"That's another great example, Ted. Perhaps people need more of those real-life examples. Otherwise, people struggle to figure it out. The children from those successful marriages have a head start on life," Andrea said.

I confirmed her statement. "They do," I said. "I've met quite a few people who grew up with parents who were successful entrepreneurs."

"How much did those millionaire couples talk about chemistry?" Kelly asked.

"Ha!!! The magical, mystical, makings of chemistry. The very thing that makes people lazy and irresponsible in relationships."

"What? You think so, Ted? How can chemistry make someone lazy and irresponsible? It is one of the major building blocks of successful relationships. Everyone knows that. Are you going to tell us to kill chemistry now?" Tasha lightly chuckled resting her glass on the arm of her chair.

"Common sense, huh? If people really understood chemistry, they would know that it couldn't be relied on," I remarked.

"I gotta hear this one now," Tasha said.

"As an example, if you see someone who meets your ideal of a significant other, you are most likely going to be very open to them," I explained. "You will be available immediately compared to seeing someone who is not your ideal. Where does that come from? Remember the radio station I mentioned?"

"You and this radio station. Let's hear it!" Susan's comment was answered by laughter from the other women in the room.

"We all have a radio station playing in our head. The station is really a network of conversations we have recorded throughout our entire lives. It tells us what is good and bad, beautiful and ugly, or smart and dumb. The station is constantly playing. As soon as we see someone who meets the conversation the radio station is playing, the station tells us if we are attracted to the person or not. If the station says the person meets the criteria, we are open to hear everything they have to say. If their face, clothes, speech patterns, intelligence, etc. all match the radio station, the brain fires off neurochemicals, and we have feelings for the person. Then we claim it was the mystical chemistry. On the other hand, if the person does not match what we hear on the radio station, we claim there is no chemistry. Their face, voice, clothes, speech patterns, etc. are either unfamiliar or they match someone our station deems as negative.

"However, when the person who meets the image on the station starts to do things that conflict with the ideas or conversations on the station, we say the chemistry has died. Likely, we have no idea the radio station is directing and guiding everything, including expectations of our significant other. If the person follows the script that was given to us on the radio station, we find them appealing. We say they understand us. As you can see, this isn't chemistry at all. Your brain is firing off all kinds of hormones and chemicals that are being completely directed by conversations you have with yourself. The other person has done nothing to earn it. It's the voices from your radio station. If I destroyed the radio station, you would have nothing called chemistry. If you didn't depend on the radio station, you would have to spend time with the person to discover if they are compatible with you. Then you will learn there is no such thing as chemistry. It is your effort and openness that makes any relationship work. If you are closed and wait for the other person to show you 'what they got,' nothing will happen.

"What I'm saying is that nothing happens until you say it will. Love, great relationships, open mindedness all happen when you tell yourself it will happen. In most cases, the radio station will tell you when it will happen. If you listen closely to the radio station, you will discover the voices are not yours. They are the voices of friends, family, movies, books, teachers, etc. The voice can belong to a random stranger that you met on the street and never saw again. Your brain stores everything. In some rare cases, it is you who decides without input from the radio station. Outside of those rare cases, the radio dominates your life.

"For those who believe there is no radio station in their mind, you are an example of the radio station telling you that you are exempt. The radio station wants to perpetually survive. Therefore, it will deceive you into believing it is not there. It will do anything and everything to protect itself, including deceive you. It does not care about breakthroughs or extraordinary relationships. It only wants to persist as it is. If someone attempts to turn it off, it will attack that person, even if the person is you.

"The most interesting part of the radio station is that you have come to believe it is you. That is like you getting in your car and not being able to distinguish between you and your car. You believe you are your car. In our common-sense world, it seems ridiculous to believe you are your car. You are taught to distinguish between self as a person and your car as a machine. Yet, you are not taught to distinguish that the voices in your head are not yours. If you listen closely, you will hear your brother saying 'you can't do it.' Or your teacher saying, 'you'll never be good at math.' Or you'll hear the person in the movie saying, 'all men cheat.' Now you believe those voices are your very own creation, when in fact, you had nothing to do with them. The cold truth is that the voices own you."

"It seems you want to destroy everything that is good about relationships. People have come to rely on chemistry. That is what makes relationships hot and steamy. Now you come along and pour water on chemistry. There may be many people who don't care for your brutally blunt communication, even if they understand what you are saying," Susan said.

"I can see that. It seems people would rather stay with something, even if it doesn't work well. It's better than changing to something you don't know how to use. People avoid uncertainty. That doesn't happen because people are not smart. They simply have these neural paths in the brain that are so engrained that it literally gives them a headache to create a new path. Headaches and uncertainty are not a favorite for most. So, I understand."

"Sounds like the radio station concept is a trap that we can't get out of. What do we do? Should we create another station or build a new radio?" Andrea asked.

"While there is no silver bullet approach. If there were a one-line answer, it would be to destroy the radio station," I replied.

"What?! You don't mean that Ted, do you? You mean change it. People are taught to learn to listen to the voice in their head." Leslie was not convinced.

I looked at her, knowing that she believed what she was saying. But I too, understood the shock of what I was saying to her and the group. "No. I said destroy it," I insisted.

"And you meant it, huh?" Tasha said knowingly.

"I only said destroy it. For one, everything on the radio station is made up. Remember, at one time, someone made up that the earth was flat. That was a conversation playing on the radio station for many years. You are trained to believe most of what's on the radio station is true. You accept it without question. Later you learn it wasn't true. There are so many things that were facts of life in the past. Now we know better. Whether those things are true or false, they are part of the radio station.

"If you think about that, everything on the station means nothing, until you give it meaning. If someone calls you beautiful, it means nothing if your radio station says you're ugly. The same goes if someone calls you ugly but you believe you're beautiful. You and I accept so much from the radio station that it's like we are put into a trance by it. If someone with credibility from Harvard or Yale says the world is a certain way, most people accept it and that one-person shaped reality until someone demonstrates otherwise. We don't question what the expert says. We trust their credentials and promote their message. That's like tranquilized thinking. The radio station is like a tranquilizer. If everyone else believes it, it must be true. So, if I destroy the tranquilizer, I destroy tranquilized thinking. Once the radio station is destroyed, people will have to distinguish thinking from having thoughts. Thinking is thinking that which is unthought or that which you have never thought. Having thoughts is the result of remembering what you saw, read, or heard. You can organize thoughts in new combinations. However, that would be an improvement based on what you already know. Thinking requires you to explore that which you don't know you don't know. The radio station does not take you into that domain. The radio station is filled with preexisting conversations.

"Many people say thinking and having thoughts are a matter of semantics. When people are unable to distinguish things, they say everything is like everything else. They lack distinctions. A martial arts master can distinguish different forms or styles of martial arts. The average person only sees fighting martial arts style. They are unable to see the different forms. It is the same with thinking and having thoughts," I explained.

"Okay, radio station destroyer!" Andrea let out a laugh. The group joined her.

"Without the radio station, you are free to think for yourself," I said.

"I'm sure there are many who will disagree. Some would say you are talking about intuition. Intuition is the voice in your head," Susan managed to stop laughing.

"I'll never dismiss intuition," I said. "That's a different conversation. At the same time, how many times have you heard someone say they had intuition about their spouse being the right person? Later they divorce that same person. I assert the choice of a spouse has more to do with the radio station. Otherwise, there would be no divorce.

"From another perspective, what you said sounds like something the radio station would say. Like I said, it wants to survive. Anything that threatens its existence is the enemy. Therefore, it will disagree. However, there are times the radio station is inappropriate, irrelevant, or obsolete. For example, the radio station tells you to worry about something that never happened and never will happen. Yet, that voice in your head about worry shapes your actions. How many couples have had serious arguments because they were worried their spouse would do something? These are the misunderstandings that happen throughout relationships of any kind. So, I'm not saying you change to another station or build a new radio. I'm saying you step outside of the radio station because it is unable to support you and your intentions."

"Well that sounds interesting. So, what are you listening to? Is that like a void? Is that when life becomes empty or depressing?" Susan asked.

"Quite to the contrary," I said. "What I'm going to say may sound strange. When you get into the zone, it's kind of like you're thinking about nothing. When you're in the zone, the radio station carries obsolete conversations. It's your intentions that drive your actions, instead of the radio station."

"Tell me more about that?" Susan said.

"Sure. Unfortunately, many times it happens in extreme crises. It could be a death in the family, natural disaster, car falling on a child, or something like that. The radio station is filled with presuppositions about what you can and cannot do. When you're in that zone, there is only your intention. There is no time or space for the radio station to inform you. You act on intention.

"For example, Andrea, you and I have lost both our parents. We both made decisions that were not built into our everyday lives. We did things that may be considered extraordinary. We were in the zone. The intention to support loved ones was the only intention and nothing could stop us. It's just like the mother lifting the car off her child. In the normal course of events, the same woman could not lift the same car because the radio station told her that it is not possible. With her child under the car, the radio station is gone. There is only intention. All your beliefs disappear.

Athletes do this all the time. When they are on the field, they are in the zone to accomplish something—win the game or make the play. This especially happens when you see the athlete do something extraordinary. After the game, if you ask the athlete how they made the play, they do not have a logical explanation for it. If they are honest, they will tell you that it was like an outer body experience."

"Okay. I can absolutely relate to that. When I lost my parents, I dropped everything. While it wasn't logical, it was the best decision for me. I wouldn't trade it if I had the chance to do it over," Andrea followed my statement.

"That I understand," I said.

"I know you do," she remarked.

"What I'm also saying, ladies, is that the radio station is something we all inherit by a certain age. The radio station is a set of conversations you inherit from your environment. The environment dictates the frequency or kinds of conversations played on the radio station. For example, one environment constantly talks about scarcity. In that environment, wealth and opportunity are difficult to find. People talk about what can't be done or what someone won't allow them to do. It's common to find frustration, anger, and disappointment in the scarcity frequency.

"In the environments that speak abundance, wealth, and opportunity are everywhere. They have conversations about learning, possibilities with resources, collaboration, vacations, new businesses, etc. Now imagine the tone of a love relationship in a scarce environment contrasted with a love relationship in an abundant environment. If you had a choice, I assume most would choose abundance.

"At the same time, if you transfer a person from scarcity to abundance, they will still believe life has limits. Initially they will bring the scarcity conversations with them, even though the environment has changed. This is especially prevalent when they encounter problems or challenges. Over time, they will make the adjustment. If they do the work, which is to transform their mindset, the transition will happen faster and smoother. The same goes for the person being transferred from abundance to scarcity. Initially they will seek opportunities in the scarcity environment. However, if opportunity is intentionally suppressed, they will eventually become frustrated, angry and disappointed. This is primarily the reason people from higher socioeconomic classes marry other affluent people. If they don't, the person in the higher socioeconomic class will have to be patient with the transformation of their significant other from a lower socioeconomic class," I said.

"Does that mean the person from the scarcity environment has to get rid of their radio station?" Tasha posed another question.

"It's great if people do that. It takes an enormous amount of work to do that. Most likely they will simply switch frequencies. They will have a new station. At the same time, there is common ground for the scarcity and abundant stations. Getting rid of the station would have you in the zone full time. When someone is in the zone full time, they will have a thought process that sounds like a pipe dream to the scarcity mindset. Most people would have a difficult time understanding a person without a radio station. They would sound like they are from another planet," I stated.

"Maybe it's time for people on this planet to start thinking like they are from another planet. Maybe that would end the number of struggles people have in relationships," Kelly said.

"That's a good point Kelly, and you opened something else. Whenever two people come together, there is bound to be misunderstandings. How you handle those misunderstandings determines the health of the relationship. Anyone can do well when life is good. How do you handle yourself, lover, and opportunity when you are not getting what you want from life? Too often people become moody, angry, and frustrated when life doesn't go the way they want. That's more of the scarcity mindset. What I'm saying is if you have the scarcity mindset and you have a misunderstanding with your significant other, you are likely to be frustrated and angry with them. You may demand you need time alone at that moment.

"However, life happens in real time. It is best to deal with things when they happen," I said. "Some call it coping skills. Some don't take the time alone, and they start yelling and/or become physically abusive. This is a paradigm that would make any relationship difficult. That kind of relationship creates a mindset that can easily miss other opportunities. Your life would be preoccupied with unresolved problems in your personal life. While some believe that having a difficult spouse makes you stronger, it doesn't. It is likely to make you defensive. I raise this because if people first acknowledge one another they would take the time to hear what the other has to say. More importantly, they would make the effort to understand what they are saying and where they are coming from. In most cases, they will find relationship conflict was a simple misunderstanding that could have been easily resolved by talking it through. I wish people understood that whatever they practice today is what they will do tomorrow. If they practice yelling and screaming in a relationship because they don't listen, they will do the same in their career and family life.

So, if they practice listening and talking things through in their love relationship, they will bring that to their professional and family life. It's really that simple."

"I guess that depends on the frequency of their radio stations," Susan said.

"Yes, it does. Now imagine no radio station. Conflict resolution would be extremely simple. Most upsets are a response to the past. When someone says something, it will make you happy or upset. It will depend on what past incident it reminds you of. The radio station informs you how to deal with it. Without the station, you can listen or watch without judgment based on past occurrences."

Susan clasped her hands in front of her face and let out a slow sigh. "These are good points," she said, "because conflict does require great communication from all parties."

"It does," I agreed. "Earlier I talked about the ability to negotiate with your spouse. Negotiation requires you to understand what the other person wants. That requires great listening without presuppositions. If people would listen to one another, they will find relationships are very easy. People get stuck with the way they did things in their family when growing up. As an adult, at some point, you create your own life. The most extraordinary relationships are the result of two people creating it from nothing. It is kind of like they are in the zone. They don't care what the rest of the world is doing. It is their life, and they can make up the rules according to what they want to experience with one another. To do that, it's important to get comfortable with talking about everything, including the uncomfortable stuff."

"That gets us back to love, affection, and acknowledgement," Leslie began to speak. "It seems everything really does lead back to that. To talk it through in the way you are saying, it is in your best interest to acknowledge one another as individual human beings. And when you talk to one another, you need to have affection in the way you speak and listen. That implies caring, and love is a big part of what the relationship—or as you called it, the 'third person'—is made of. Both people contribute love to that third person. If they do that, the third person survives and so does the relationship."

"Well said, Leslie," I commended. "You could have just said that, and the book would have been done. I gave the long version."

"No," she said. "There was a lot of necessary background for us to get to this point in the conversation. If someone walked in on this, they would be lost. This conversation was a journey. The journey is often more valuable than the destination."

"For sure," I agreed.

"There's another way it seems acknowledgement works. Since we all have been given a radio station, denying it only makes things worse. As you said, the radio station is programmed to avoid anything that would threaten its survival. Therefore, it will remain invisible and say it does not exist. So, it is imperative to acknowledge the radio station. If you don't, you're like the alcoholic who denies they drink too much," Kelly added.

"That's a great point, and alcoholism is a good example. The more you resist the more it persists," I remarked.

"So, the radio station can intoxicate you. Then you drive drunk into someone's life claiming you want love from them. So, the radio station defines love, even if it really isn't love. If the radio station believes it's love, it will defend itself," Tasha said.

"That's a great analogy! Sounds a little insane, doesn't it?" I shook my head looking at Tasha. "You are taught that driving drunk is dangerous. Meanwhile, you are intoxicated by a radio station that has you recklessly drive through another person's life. If you have the scarcity mindset, you are even more dangerous. What you are also pointing out is the elements that are parts of the radio station. People want to be right or make wrong, justify, defend, etc. A person will defend their version of love as right. Then they invalidate yours. If you attempt to show them another way to express love, they may believe you are trying to dominate them. So, they must avoid being dominated. And that is the situation people often find themselves in."

"Exactly!" Andrea said. "You also mentioned third party interference. That would seem to be the time people seek support from friends or family who may or may not have their best interest in mind. If they don't have their best interest in mind, they will give poor advice. If they do have their best interest, they could still give poor advice because they don't have all the details. They only have their friend's side of the story. To your point, it is better when people learn to talk things through. And they should always remember that listening to one another is the most important part of communication. While listening, it is wise to acknowledge the radio station may be giving bad advice also. So, it's important to acknowledge to one another that their radio station is saying don't believe the other and/or fight to be right. What a vicious cycle. No wonder relationships seem so hard. You really need to practice this stuff to become good at it. But you said, what you practice today is what you will do tomorrow. How very true. Now I can really see how being in the zone with your significant other is important. The two of you must create a world of your own. It's like being present to one another all the time, instead of being controlled by the radio station!" Andrea looked around the room. She stopped at me and smiled. "I'm catching on, Ted. Perhaps the student will become the teacher."

"That's a great way to put it," I said. "And making love is one easy way for couple to get into the zone."

"You always get those extra sex plugs in there," she laughed.

"Yeah, he does," Tasha managed to say.

Andrea continued, "So I guess being in the zone is one way to get rid of the radio station."

"That's a way to see it. However, there is another side to the radio station. Up to now, it may seem as though I'm saying the radio station gives negative messages. What I'm really saying is that everything is connected to that station."

"I can see that. At least I think so," Andrea's forehead wrinkled with thought. "What do you mean?" she asked.

"I'll give you an example that may make some people unhappy. Let's suppose I'm in a relationship with a woman who really loves me. And let's say we've been in a relationship for two years. Now, I come home, get on one knee, and present her with a two-carat emerald-cut, flawless diamond ring along with a dozen roses. How do you think she will feel?"

"Is that a trick question?" Susan asked.

"This is one of those stay with me conversations," I remarked.

"We're trying, Ted!" Tasha said, adding more laughter to the conversation.

Smiling, Susan added, "Unless you've done something wrong, and you are trying to make up, she will be very happy. I would think most women would be happy with two carats, even though I don't necessarily think carat size is a true measure of love."

"That's a fair thing to say. Except, you gave two possible responses a woman could have. One, he did something wrong. Two, she simply believes he loves her and wants to marry her. Yes?" I looked around the room to see if everyone was still with me.

Susan spoke for the group, "Correct," she said.

"Let's look at the reality of the situation. The reality is I come home, get on one knee, give her a rock, and dead plants."

"You're being a little extreme with this. Or maybe you're being a smart ass again. Is that the smart ass frequency your station plays?" Andrea asked.

"I think all the women in this room will agree that it's an acceptable norm for a man to propose this way. It's part of our social construct. Right ladies?" Susan looked around the room. The women shook their heads in agreement.

"Is it?" I asked. "Is it normal to be happy when a man gives a woman a rock that someone found in a mine and flowers that are dead because they have been cut from their source of life? The flowers are dead. It will just take a couple of days for her to realize that. And the rock? What's the difference between the rock I buy in the store and the one I find in the backyard? Why can't she be happy if I find a rock in the yard and give her dandelions I picked in a field? What's the difference?"

"In a woman's mind, there is a big difference," Andrea answered.

"Is it really the woman's mind? Or is it one of the conversations or frequencies on the radio station? Technically speaking, there is no difference between the rock in the yard and the diamond some person found deep in dirt. The radio station is the only thing that tells her the difference. If you doubt me, give a newborn a rock from your backyard and a diamond, they will show you if there's a difference. They have not had the radio station imposed on them yet. The radio station tells you when to be happy, sad, or rebellious."

"Now you're just taking the fun out of life. What's wrong with being happy over a diamond ring and flowers, Ted?" Susan asked.

"I never said there is something wrong with that. Likely, the woman believes the diamond is an expression of my love. How can a diamond and flowers represent my love? That's no different than believing you can have a love affair with a picture of someone. The person in the picture is an image in the same way the diamond is an image of love. Love is between two people. If I came home to the same woman and said I give myself to you and want to spend the rest of my life with you, what might her radio station say? Would it say put a ring on my finger if you want that? How can a rock and dead flowers be more valuable than me? In a way, that's an insult to all human beings. Have we really been usurped by material possessions?"

"You have a major point there," Tasha said. "There is no one size fits all. We are all different and yet the same—especially when it comes to life ventures that will naturally happen to us. Some examples are, birth, death, food, clothing, shelter, and living daily among people. Therefore, our life-style values will play a major role in the level of appreciation for diamond and the diamond in the ruff from the backyard. My question is: Are your values focused on human relationships or materialism? Maybe most women are not taught to appreciate what you are saying. Like you said, we are all listening to the radio station."

"Right. Well I'm not saying a diamond in the rough from the backyard. I'm saying any rock lying on the ground," I added. "So, if her radio station says 'he doesn't love you if he doesn't put a ring on it,' she will justify being upset. She may even invalidate me. Perhaps she would be embarrassed to tell her friends and family that I never presented a ring. That would be a woman who is more concerned with looking good and avoiding looking bad to others. At that point, love has gone out the window. That is all the doing of the radio station. As you can see, the idea of love is built into the radio station. So, it is not love she has for me. It is a representation of love based on the commands of her radio station. In fact, she may not love me at all. I may simply fit the image that is part of her radio frequency. She would be in a relationship with the frequency from the radio station, instead of me. A two-carat, flawless, emerald diamond ring may be the right frequency to make her believe she is happy."

"Okay," Andrea said, looking at me. "You kind of just destroyed the whole idea of love. Are you saying there is no such thing as love now? It's just some idea in our head that is playing on the radio station?"

I laughed along with the women in the room.

"Don't kill the messenger," I said.

"It's not me you need to be worried about. It's all the people who believe or hope for the fairytale love," she warned.

"You can only love to the extent the radio station allows you to love. Beyond that, there is probably confusion or fear," I replied.

"What? Wait," Kelly threw both hands in the air. "So," she said, "you are saying whatever frequency love plays on your radio station, is the level of love you can experience? Are you saying you can't experience love outside of the frequency playing in your head?"

"That's a good way to put it," I said.

Susan looked over at Andrea, "Then you can just change frequencies. That would be like changing the radio station to one that plays music you like. Or you can try listening to music you've never heard," she said.

"Yes. That is our paradigm. You are taught to do more, better, different, of the same thing. The more things change, the more they stay the same. You see. In the scenario where I come home with the diamond and flowers, the woman presupposed she should be happy. Technically a rock and dead flowers are no reason to be happy. However, her station or frequency informed her to be happy. If she changes frequencies, I may have to give her some other token to be happy. That's the same thing but a different token."

"Yeah, but..." Susan paused. Waving her hand, she continued, "Okay. I see what you mean."

"Yeah, but what?" I urged.

"I got it," she said. "I don't really like it, but I got it. Please, keep going."

"It's not so easy to express what I'm saying," I said. "The English language has too many limits. I would literally have to invent new distinctions in language to express it."

85

"Would that new language also revamp relationships in general, especially as we understand it today?" Tasha asked.

"It could easily have that effect. Let me put it this way. I want to make this short. There are ancient civilizations that have been found. Those civilizations have no signs of warfare. What kind of education would people have to receive to have no signs of warfare? The Olmecs is one such civilization. They were here in the Americas, including the US. Another recent discovery of an ancient city with no signs of warfare was found outside of Turkey. It is called Gobeki Tempi and believed to be about 13,000 years old. It would seem the Olmecs and people of Gobeki Tempi had a very different way to relate to one another. Because we have not figured out how to live without war, there may be many things our culture is incapable of understanding.

"Another example in modern times is Japanese Kaizen. It is a way the Japanese work together in the workforce. It is responsible for constant improvement. The US has attempted to use Kaizen. Except, US culture does not know how to support the concept. Therefore, it fails here, or we are unable to produce the same results as the Japanese.

"With all that said, I am saying there is a good chance 'love' as we know it may be a poor translation of what western culture attempted to understand when they encountered indigenous cultures around the world. Perhaps there was nothing in their language that could comprehend the way human beings lived together when they existed without wars. The closest they could come up with is 'love.' People do that all the time. When they can't really grasp what you are saying, they say, 'Oh, that is just like…' They attempt to make it fit their reality, instead of asking questions to fully understand it. In many cases, it is in your best interest to immerse yourself in the other's culture and 'become that culture' to fully understand and appreciate it. Then you may find it is untranslatable because it is a very different paradigm. And it is a completely different way of thinking and living.

"What if those ancient cultures did not relate to one another as physical bodies or objects? What if they related to one another as human beings? In western culture, we objectify everything, even the idea of God. And we love or destroy objects. When we see one another as objects, it is easy to hurt one another. If we knew how to just 'be there' with one another that may be something like being in the zone with one another. Then a rock and dead flowers could never replace or represent a human being. Love would be an expression from one person to another, instead of from one object to a person."

"Now that's kind of profound. It makes you really think," Tasha said. "So, can I trade in my radio station for that?" Tasha leaned back in her chair. Her warm laughter filled the room. The ensemble of women joined her with their own brand of declarations.

Although I warned the women of my coming thoughts, each woman seemingly managed to seriously consider what I had to say. Our laughter came at perfect times to lighten the mood; this time was no different, so I joined them.

"You make it sound like you're buying a car," I said. "I wouldn't say trade," I went on to explain. "It takes work. It's really a matter of stripping away the radio station layer after layer. It seems the more of the radio station you strip away the more you learn who you really are. It's like the you that you really are is covered with layers of dust that society imposed on you from the day you were born. That dust is just voices I called a radio station."

"So how do you peel off the layers?" Andrea asked.

"That may be counterintuitive," I said. "You confront it. You address every aspect of your radio station. As you confront it, you begin to hear whom the voices belong to. You also hear that the radio station is the result of choices you made as a child. Because those voices have been with you since childhood, you believe it is who you really are. To do that, you need the proper tools. It's not an automatic or magical thing that happens. There is an intention to free yourself from a you that was never you.

"I can't emphasize more that you have to do the work, even if it is uncomfortable. The more of the radio station you peel away the more freedom you have to be yourself. Could you imagine a relationship where fight, flight, or freeze are eliminated or significantly reduced? How free would that feel? What would that relationship look like?

"Great questions. I'm calling you when I have relationship problems," Susan said.

"Most likely I will ask you a bunch of questions," I remarked. "I'm not so good at giving advice. Questions help you discover things that are not immediately obvious to you."

"I can see that. But sometimes you just want the answer," Susan admitted. "You don't want to think too hard, especially when you're stressed out over someone you love or want to love."

"Yeah, look at all the talking you've been doing tonight," Kelly added.

"I asked a lot of questions, too," I said.

"You talked a lot, though. I'm not saying too much. You just said a lot of stuff. It was good because it made me think differently. I think I'll have a different approach to relationships now. I'm calling you, too, when I have a problem," Andrea said.

"Some things required me to talk," I said. "Take the radio station, for example. I had to lay it out. For the most part, I laid out a different way to look at something. That made you ask questions. Then I could ask more questions. Many times, the question can be more valuable than the answer. Questions can put your mind on a journey."

"Well, I have a question," Tasha said, looking at me and Andrea.

"What's that?" I asked.

"Since you have all this knowledge and know what questions to ask, why aren't you married?" Tasha seemingly asked the question everyone wanted an answer to.

Andrea raised her eyebrows confirming her curiosity. While Kelly, rested her chin in the palm of her hand awaiting my answer.

Leslie added her acknowledgement, "Yes, why is that?"

Susan leaned forward, retrieving her glass from the table. "We're waiting my friend," she said.

"Wow! You love getting right to it, don't you?" I directed my answer to Tasha, who simply smiled. "You've asked great and very personal questions tonight," I added.

"I am learning from you," she teased.

I chuckled.

"What's the matter?" Tasha continued. "I asked you a question you can't answer?" Her smile broadened.

"I'll answer you," I said.

"I'm listening," Tasha egged me on.

"Yeah, me too," Susan remarked.

" I think I already know what he will say girls." Andrea looked at me with a half-smile.

I looked at her, giving her an upward nod. I asked, "What will I say?"

"Oh no," she replied, "I'm not helping you. You've been asking us all the tough questions. Now it's your turn to answer some tough questions." A full smile spread across her face as she looked in my direction. The capacity of these ladies to bring a touch of lightheartedness to a serious subject was encouraging.

"You ladies have been asking personal questions all night, especially you, Tasha," I said.

"Me!" Tasha feigned surprise, as laughter engulfed the room.

"Enough!" Andrea said sternly. "Let's hear it. Why aren't you married, Mr. Relationship Expert?"

I continued to laugh, "I never said I was a relationship expert. I have a good understanding of how to create great dynamics in any relationship. To answer your question, it takes something to be in a relationship with me."

"What does that mean?" Leslie's voice flattened." Does that mean all of your good advice goes out the window when you're in a relationship with someone? I need clarity."

"Don't help him. I want to hear what he has to say." Leaning forward, Andrea looked in my direction, insisting that I answer.

"To your question, Leslie, no. I'm saying that I'm very demanding. First, I need a woman who is open enough to talk about anything, even if it's uncomfortable for her. I'm not going to eat her discomfort around a certain subject. She will have to handle it and talk."

"Is that you being cold again?" Leslie asked.

"No. Not at all. It's a relationship between adults. Whatever the discomfort is, it will not go away by avoiding it. Let's put it on the table."

"Okay," she said, "keep going."

"Not every woman is comfortable with that," I stated. "They may equate that with controlling. How can I take a woman seriously if she is incapable of having a conversation? It's only talking."

Susan spoke up, "You're saying no woman in the world is willing to talk to you about everything?"

"No. I never said that," I replied. "I said that is something I need. At the same time, as deep as I can go in conversation, there is a shallow side to me."

"I was waiting for this part," Andrea relaxed in her chair.

"So, you already know, huh?" I asked.

"Keep going," she said.

"Are we making you squirm now, Ted?" Tasha asked.

"No, not at all. The shallow side of me is about taking care of yourself. While it's important to have a well-maintained body, it is equally as important to invest time in developing your mind. With that said, I've met women who were intelligent and very open to any conversation. Except, they allowed themselves to become overweight. I haven't met an available woman who has done both."

"Maybe you're looking for perfection," Susan added.

"Why can't you help the overweight woman lose weight? If she loves you, she wouldn't have a problem losing weight for you. Maybe she just needs the support. You can be the catalyst for her to lose weight," Kelly suggested.

"I can see why you would say that. I can even see how you could say my radio station is looking for a woman who is physically and mentally developed," I said. "That would be a fair thing for all of you to say. I get that. My one concern revolves around a woman's ability to support me in a relationship. To your point, Kelly, if she wanted to lose weight, she would have done it already. That has to be her commitment. There is no reason for her to do it for me. She needs to do it for herself. No woman is under obligation to do anything for me, including losing weight. It has to be her choice."

"Maybe no one cared before," Kelly added.

"It's her body. She is the only one that needs to care for it," I said. "Everyone gets one body. Your body is your responsibility. If you don't care for it, who else will? Besides, sometimes people believe they did something for you, so now you owe them. Those are not the greatest dynamics to have in a relationship. And, Susan, it's not perfection I'm seeking. It is someone who will understand how to support me. If a woman is not committed to continuously developing her mind, she may believe that I think too much. I am constantly learning new things. Some are completely unrelated to my profession. It could be science, art, social sciences, technology, etc. Learning new things facilitates my intellectual development.

Furthermore, in my professional life, it makes me more valuable to clients when I can connect unrelated topics to their industry. It helps to offer new perspectives. Not every woman knows how to support a man who thinks that way."

Andrea nodded." I can see that," she said.

"And I prefer a woman have a similar commitment to developing her body. Body and mind go hand in hand for me. Now that doesn't mean she has to be a competitive athlete. She needs to be able to emotionally support me when I want to physically exercise my body. There are women who will say they are comfortable with her man gaining weight. She may be comfortable with both of them gaining weight together. That mindset would not be supportive for me. So, I have not met a woman who clearly demonstrated physical and mental commitment to development. I need them both."

"It sounds like you won't help a woman develop one or both," Kelly said.

"I never said never. A commitment to both requires a certain mindset. It's the mindset that is more important to me. It's her mindset that allows her to be supportive of me. By the way, international travel is included in mental development."

"You exclude an enormous number of women up front," Tasha said.

"Usually it's the guy who approaches the woman," I continued. "When it comes to physical attraction, my radio station looks for a certain appeal. I'm not so concerned with height. I'm 5'6." I've dated women as short as 5'0" and as tall as 6'2." Their height never made me uncomfortable. My preference is a woman who is physically fit. Since I'm the one approaching, I do look for a certain attractiveness in the face. If women approached men, there would be a greater chance of me meeting a larger pool of women. Since it's up to me, I set the criteria. Unfortunately, many are eliminated. For the record, I've seen many physically attractive women who were not appealing to me. I've approached women who were giving me a shy stare. When I said a simple 'hello,' she demonstrated a very ugly attitude. Social skills are also important to me. So, Tasha, to answer your question, it's physical attractiveness first. That gets my interest. To keep my interest, I need high intelligence. I mention that knowing high intelligence can be developed with exposure. And I look for a mindset that is committed to constant development of mind and body. I have not met a woman who consistently offers both. Included in that is integrity. It's important that she can keep her word. Whatever agreements she and I have are between us. I expect her to keep them. If she is unable to keep her word, she needs to let me know. That way I can make a sound decision on how I want to move forward. Some women may see that as demanding." I paused, and looking at Tasha, I asked, "Did I answer your question?"

"You did," she replied. "And you're saying there are no beautiful woman with high intelligence."

"I would *never* say that. I've met some. They were already married or in a relationship. I think I met a couple of beautiful women who presented themselves as intelligent. However, they said they were in relationships when, in fact, they were not. That's an integrity issue. Why would you start things off with a lie? Is that to make it appear there is demand for you?"

"Some women get approached a lot," Susan said.

"If you have a one-size-fits-all response to men, the only men you will attract are the men who are attracted to that response. If you want to attract a different type of man, learn who your audience is and what is appealing to them. If you want to attract a Rolls Royce, don't use marketing tactics for a person who can only afford a Honda Civic."

Smiles and laughter spread across the room.

"So," I briefly concluded, "what do you ladies think of this conversation?"

Susan was the first to answer. "You gave me a lot to think about," she said." The radio station concept is deep. I must watch how I react now. From what you said, you allow yourself to be attracted to whomever you want, and you feel no guilt or shame about it. So, I'm not going to feel guilty about what attracts me either. You said you are shallow when it comes to looks. Ha ha! I'm going to be shallow, too."

"Well, my intention is to offer the same as I am seeking from her," I replied. "What about you, Tasha?"

"I also think it was a deep conversation. I liked the stuff you said about the radio station," Tasha said.

"I think you just gave us a group therapy session," Andrea added. "How much do we owe you?" Andrea feigned seriousness, as another smile warmed her expression, and the other ladies laughed in agreement."

I smiled as well. "Wait," I said, "let Tasha finish,"

"Okay, sorry," Andrea gave a light apology looking in Tasha's direction.

Tasha's warm personality would not allow her to be offended. "That's okay," she said, smiling at Andrea." I also think it was a therapy session. It really has me thinking. The thing that got me the most was the idea of killing trust. That's like wow! Who would ever think of that? You think about stuff that most people never think of."

"Right?" Kelly remarked. "Everyone is taught to trust or mistrust."

"Exactly! Either I trust you or I don't. Whoever thought of killing trust? If I do that, I never have to worry about trust again. That's deep," Tasha continued." So, I think you would make a great husband, Ted. You know how to bring a lot out of people. Well, I'll speak for myself. It seems you know how to make a woman feel comfortable discussing anything. I would think most women would like that."

"Are you about to drop to one knee and propose?" I asked.

Laughter quickly filled the room.

Mid-laugh, Susan continued the teasing, "Yes," she said, "she is going to pull out that two-carat, flawless, emerald-cut diamond ring for you, Ted."

Tasha rested her head in her hand nodding in disingenuous frustration. "No, I'm not saying that," she paused, "and I left the ring home." She smiled. "Seriously," she added, "I just think you would be good for the right woman. I enjoyed this conversation. I want to try and kill trust and see how that works. I just need a guy who is open enough."

"He also needs high integrity," I said. "It's helpful if he's committed to honoring his word with you. Thank you, by the way."

"Is it okay if I speak now?" Andrea asked, looking at us both.

"You finished, Tasha?" I inquired.

"Yes. Your turn Andrea," Tasha replied.

"Like I said, this was a therapy session for me," Andrea said. "I think you should do a workshop and include all the things you've said. Sometimes we ladies need to hear another perspective from a man. Many of the things you said made a lot of sense. At first, I didn't like some of the stuff you said."

"Like what?" I asked.

"You said so much stuff. I don't remember everything I didn't like," Andrea admitted. "But, when you first started talking about being tough and independent, I first thought 'oh, he just can't handle a tough and independent woman.' Then you continued, and it started making sense. How can you have love and toughness together? They don't go together. And if you want to be partners in this journey in life, you need to learn to work together. Telling your man, you are independent, and you don't need him is not a good way to work together. In fact, you are probably pushing him away. I think it was good because you seem like you can be trusted, and you have good intentions. That probably makes you good marriage material." She laughed, "Maybe not for me though. I don't care about working out. Like you said, you're demanding. I like that you gave us a man's perspective. I think women are accustomed to listening to other women. It's good to hear a man speak openly and honestly. It forces us ladies to rethink our own beliefs about relationships. So, you just need to do a workshop. I'll attend it."

"Thanks," I said. Looking at Leslie, I added, "How about you, Leslie?"

"I knew I would be next," she remarked. "Oh, I have so many thoughts. I guess the thing that stuck out most was the radio station. Personally, I have a lot of thoughts in my head. Sometimes I second-guess myself. Now I can see how some of those voices are not mine. That can be annoying sometimes. I want to go right, but the voice in my head says 'go left.' That was my mother saying 'don't do that.' Later I find that going right was the best thing for me. I would love to kill that radio station! It has probably sabotaged relationships with a couple of good men. I also think it may have stopped me from one or two great career moves."

"Wow!" I exclaimed. "That's good! This stuff is beyond intimate relationships ladies. It affects every aspect of your life, including your professional life. I'm sorry, Leslie. Were you finished?"

"Pretty much. I can see how the radio station can control your entire life," Leslie said. "It can make you afraid when there is no reason to be afraid. As women, either we look at a man as Prince Charming or we are afraid he is an axe murderer. We don't have a right to impose either onto men. Most men are not axe murderers. We ladies just have that voice playing in our heads. I would never want to be thought of and treated as an axe murderer."

"Yes, that does get a little crazy for us," I remarked facetiously. "Anything else?"

"No. I'm good," Leslie replied.

"How about you, Kelly?" I asked. "What did you get from this conversation?"

"A lot," she said. "I like the radio station stuff and killing trust. But I really thought about what I'm offering a man. You talked about the woman who was a soccer mom. We are taught that, as a woman, you must be out there slaying the dragons in the workforce. Here this woman was a soccer mom. At the same time, she was like the number one salesperson for her husband's consulting firm. It was a consulting firm, right?"

"Yes, it was," I said.

"That man's wife wasn't just his number one cheerleader; she was a champion," Kelly stated. "You said he had his largest client because of his wife?"

I nodded.

"She sounds like an amazing woman. She's not tied up in what it means to be a stay-at-home mom. She is supporting her husband in so many ways. It's like she's living with a purpose. She is probably a great mom. And she is a great wife and partner to her husband. And like you said, they moved into a bigger house."

"They did," I said, nodding in agreement.

"She contributed to that. They are a team, building something. That is also a great example for children to see. It doesn't mean their marriage is perfect. They are working together in life. Life is hard enough. The last thing you want to come home to is a spouse who works against you. This woman wasn't just in his corner. She is out in the world fighting with him. She made life easier for him. That story really stuck in my head. If we, as women, strived to be a partner like her, maybe marriages would last longer. It takes two. It sounds like he was doing his part. He was a business owner, and he took care of his home financially so his wife did not have to work. That takes pressure off her. Then she stepped up and went above and beyond being a stay-at-home mom. I loved that story. Thank you."

"You're welcome," I said and looked around the room. "I thank all of you for being so open and engaging. I enjoyed this conversation."

"So did we," Susan remarked. "I think you were the hit of the party," she added. "I knew you would be."

"It was our pleasure. You answered all of my questions!" Tasha leaned back satisfied.

"Ted's therapy session, instead of TED talks," Andrea said, laughing at herself.

Tasha shook her head sighing. That's just bad," Laughing, she said, "Really Andrea?"

Andrea threw up her hands. "I think I'm funny," she said shrugging as the other women laughed.

Kelly's eyes widened, as her smile left her face. "I have an idea," she stated.

"What's that?" I asked.

"Why don't we do this again?" she posed.

www.ingramcontent.com/pod-product-compliance
Lightning Source LLC
Chambersburg PA
CBHW071502070526
44578CB00001B/420